# Family Literacy
# for new groups

## The NFER evaluation of family literacy with linguistic minorities, Year 4 and Year 7

——————

GREG BROOKS • JOHN HARMAN

DOUGAL HUTCHISON • SALLY KENDALL • ANNE WILKIN

GW00724613

The
**Basic Skills**
Agency

Published March 1999
ISBN 1 85990 092 5
Design: Studio 21

# Contents

—————

*List of Tables*     vi

*List of Figures*     vii

*Members of the evaluation team*     viii

*Acknowledgements*     viii

**Executive Summary**     x

## Chapter

1. **Origin and aims of the study**     1
   1.1 Origin     1
   1.2 Context     2
   1.3 Aim     2
   1.4 Purpose and structure of this report     3

2. **Outline of the evaluation**     4
   2.1 Forms of information     4
   2.2 Frequency of quantitative data collection     4
   2.3 Quantitative data-collection instruments     4
   2.4 Quantitative data collected     6
   2.5 Qualitative data     6
   2.6 Comment on the Year 7 courses     7

3. **Adapting the family literacy model for linguistic minority families**     8
   3.1 General     8
   3.2 Adapting the parents' sessions     8
   3.3 Adapting the children's sessions     9
   3.4 Adapting the joint sessions     10

4. **Characteristics of the linguistic minority families**     11
   4.1 Languages and literacies     11
   4.2 Gender and ethnicity     12
   4.3 Ages     13

4.4 Parents' occupations                                                                    13
4.5 Parents' qualifications                                                                 14
4.6 Recruitment                                                                             15
4.7 Retention and attendance                                                                16

5.  **The benefits for linguistic minority parents and children**                          18
    5.1  The progress in literacy made by linguistic minority parents                       18
    5.2  Tutors' views on benefits for parents                                              20
    5.3  Parents' plans                                                                     21
    5.4  Parents' involvement with school                                                   22
    5.5  The progress in literacy made by linguistic minority children                      23
    5.6  Tutors' views on benefits for children                                             27
    5.7  Feedback from children's schools                                                   28
    5.8  Conclusions on courses for linguistic minority families                            28

6.  **Adapting the model for families with a child in Year 4**                              29
    6.1  Adapting the parents' sessions                                                      29
    6.2  Adapting the children's sessions                                                    31
    6.3  Adapting the joint sessions                                                         32

7.  **Characteristics of the families with a child in Year 4**                              35
    7.1  Gender, ethnicity and language                                                      35
    7.2  Ages                                                                                35
    7.3  Parents' occupations                                                                36
    7.4  Parents' qualifications                                                             36
    7.5  Recruitment                                                                         37
    7.6  Retention and attendance                                                            39

8.  **The benefits for Year 4 children and their parents**                                  40
    8.1  The progress in literacy made by parents of Year 4 children                         40
    8.2  Tutors' views on the benefits for parents                                           42
    8.3  Parents' plans                                                                      42
    8.4  Parents' involvement with school                                                    43
    8.5  The progress in literacy made by Year 4 children                                    44
    8.6  Conclusions on courses for families with a child in Year 4                          48

9.  **Factors contributing to the success of the programmes**                               49
    9.1  Human factors                                                                       49
    9.2  Material factors                                                                    51
    9.3  Possible barriers or challenges to the success of the Programmes                    53
    9.4  Conclusion                                                                          55

## 10. Evidence from the observations of teaching sessions    56

     10.1   Planning    56
     10.2   Clarity of objectives    57
     10.3   Use of resources    58
     10.4   Management of learning    58
     10.5   Differentiation    59
     10.6   The joint sessions    61
     10.7   Participation during separate sessions    62
     10.8   Record-keeping    62
     10.9   Conclusions from observations of teaching sessions    64

## 11. Conclusions and recommendations    65

     11.1   The three Alternative Models overall    65
     11.2   The linguistic minorities model    65
     11.3   The Year 4 model    65
     11.4   Material factors in the two models' success    66
     11.5   Human factors in the two models' success    66
     11.6   Possible barriers to success    66
     11.7   Conclusions from observations of teaching sessions    67
     11.8   Lessons and recommendations    67

## References    69

## Appendix   Full description of how the evaluation was carried out    70

     A.1   Forms of information    70
     A.2   Frequency of quantitative data collection    70
     A.3   Background information    70
     A.4   Quantitative data collected    73
     A.5   Qualitative data    73
     A.6   Comment on the evaluation of Year 7 courses    74

# List of Tables

## Chapter 2
*Table 2.1:*   Forms of information gathered                                                    4
*Table 2.2:*   Numbers of LEAs, courses, parents and children providing
              quantitative data, by Model and overall                                          6

## Chapter 4
*Table 4.1:*   Linguistic background of participants in courses for linguistic
              minority families                                                               11
*Table 4.2:*   Ethnic origins of parents and children in courses for linguistic
              minority families                                                               12
*Table 4.3:*   Age-distribution of participating linguistic minority parents
              at start of course                                                              13
*Table 4.4:*   Age-distribution of participating linguistic minority children
              at start of course                                                              13
*Table 4.5:*   Occupations of parents on courses for linguistic minority families             14
*Table 4.6:*   Highest qualifications of parents on courses for linguistic minority
              families                                                                        14
*Table 4.7:*   Attendance and retention rates on courses for linguistic
              minority families                                                               17

## Chapter 5
*Table 5.1:*   Distribution of linguistic minority parents' literacy scores                   18
*Table 5.2:*   Distribution of linguistic minority children's literacy scores                 24
*Table 5.3:*   Average standardised scores of children aged 5:00-6:01 at
              beginning of course (N=65)                                                      25

## Chapter 7
*Table 7.1:*   Age-distribution of participating Year 4 parents at start of course            35
*Table 7.2:*   Occupations of parents of Year 4 children                                      36
*Table 7.3:*   Highest qualifications of parents of Year 4 children                           37
*Table 7.4:*   Attendance and retention rates on courses for families with
              a child in Year 4                                                               39

## Chapter 8
*Table 8.1:*   Distribution of literacy scores of parents of Year 4 children                  40
*Table 8.2:*   Distribution of Year 4 children's literacy scores                              45

## Appendix
*Table A.1:*   Forms of information gathered                                                   70
*Table A.2:*   Numbers of LEAs, courses, parents and children providing
              quantitative data, by Model and overall                                         73

# List of Figures

Executive Summary
*Figure X.1:*  Linguistic minority children's gains in reading and writing                                    xi
*Figure X.2:*  Proportions of Year 4 children with literacy difficulties,
              beginning and end of course                                                                    xii

## Chapter 5
*Figure 5.1:*  Linguistic minority parents' literacy scores, beginning and end
              of course, returners only                                                                      19
*Figure 5.2:*  Linguistic minority children's writing scores, beginning and
              end of course, returners only                                                                  25
*Figure 5.3:*  Linguistic minority children's *Literacy Baseline* scores,
              beginning and end of course, returners only                                                    26

## Chapter 8
*Figure 8.1:*  Year 4 parents' literacy scores, beginning and end of course,
              returners only                                                                                 41
*Figure 8.2:*  Year 4 children's writing scores, beginning and end of course,
              returners only                                                                                 46
*Figure 8.3:*  Year 4 children's *Progress in English* scores, beginning and end
              of course, returners only                                                                      47

# Members of the evaluation team

*Dr Greg Brooks,* Senior Research Officer at NFER, Slough, was the Project Director, carried out some of the fieldwork, and was the author of all sections of this report not otherwise attributed below.

*John Harman,* consultant to NFER, based in Berkshire, carried out some of the fieldwork, and analysed and wrote up the observations of teaching sessions (chapter 10).

*Dr Dougal Hutchison,* Chief Statistician at NFER, Slough, was the project statistician.

*Sally Kendall,* Research Officer at NFER's Northern Office in York, analysed and wrote up the course tutors' views on benefits for parents and children (sections 5.2-5.4, 5.6-5.7 and 8.2-8.4).

*Anne Wilkin,* Research Officer at NFER's Northern Office in York, carried out some of the fieldwork, and analysed and wrote up the course tutors' views on adapting the model (chapters 2 and 6), recruitment (sections 4.6 and 7.5), and factors contributing to the success of the programmes (chapter 9).

# Acknowledgements

The authors wish to express their thanks to:

- colleagues at the Basic Skills Agency, for constant support

- the Adult Basic Skills and Early Years tutors in the programmes, for gathering most of the data

and especially

- all the parents and children involved, for their cooperation and willingness to be scrutinised.

# Executive Summary

―――――

## The Family Literacy Alternative Models

The original model of family literacy established by the Basic Skills Agency in 1994 was for families where the parents had basic skills needs and the children were aged three to six. Very few families from linguistic minorities participated in the Demonstration Programmes evaluated by NFER in 1994-95, and only families with a child in the relevant age range were targeted. In early 1997 the Agency implemented family literacy courses which followed three alternative models:

- working with linguistic minority families where the parents had basic skills needs and the children were aged three to six

- working with parents with basic skills needs, and their children in Year 4

- working with parents with basic skills needs, and their children in Year 7.

In most cases, these models were delivered through courses of 10 to 12 weeks' duration during school terms, though adjustments to local circumstances were envisaged. Each course was designed for up to 10 parents and 12 children.

## The evaluation

The Basic Skills Agency commissioned NFER to evaluate these alternative models in 1997-98. The aim of the evaluation was to establish whether the original model had been appropriately adapted for the new groups, and how effective courses following the new models had been. By 'effective' was meant reaching the target audience, producing learning gains for parents and children and gains in confidence, etc. Background data were gathered on parents and children participating in 47 courses. Performance data were collected at the beginning and end of their courses on the attainment in literacy of 287 parents and 344 children. Observations were made of 43 teaching sessions, and 30 course staff were interviewed.

## The three Alternative Models overall

- The attempt to adapt the original Family Literacy model for families with a child in Year 7 was largely unsuccessful. This was partly because of problems of retaining parents on the courses, and partly because of the very different circumstances of secondary schools.

- But the original model was successfully adapted both for linguistic minority families with a child aged 3 to 6, and for families with a child in Year 4.

- Successful adaptation for linguistic minorities depended on close attention to bilingual issues.

- Successful adaptation for Year 4 depended on detailed negotiation with schools, including taking account of the National Literacy Project/Strategy.

## The linguistic minorities model

- The main linguistic minority recruited was speakers of Urdu and Punjabi.

- Attendance and retention rates (89 and 86 per cent respectively) were reasonably high for the children, and quite high for the parents (75 per cent in both cases).

- The parents significantly improved their literacy in English – their average final score was 10 per cent higher than the average starting score.

- The parents' ability to help their children had improved.

- Many of the parents planned to go on further courses.

- Many had become more involved with their children's schools.

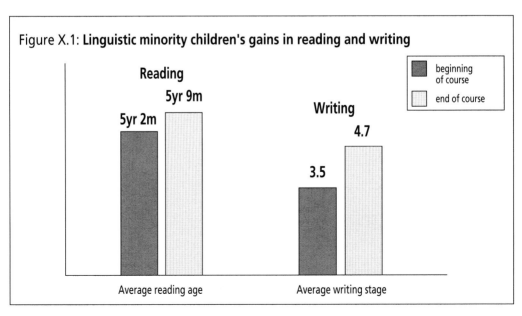

Figure X.1: **Linguistic minority children's gains in reading and writing**

- The children made substantial progress in writing and in early literacy generally – the (powerful) effect size of 0.72 represented about seven months' gain in reading age in three months, and the gain in writing was about twice as large as in the Demonstration Programmes.
- Boys and girls made approximately equal gains.
- The gains for parents were very similar to those in the Demonstration Programmes, and the gains for children were slightly larger.

## The Year 4 model

- Good relations with host schools were crucial.
- Attendance and retention rates (92 and 94 per cent respectively) were high for the children, and reasonably high for the parents (87 and 83 per cent respectively).
- The parents significantly improved their literacy– their average final score was six per cent higher than the average starting score.

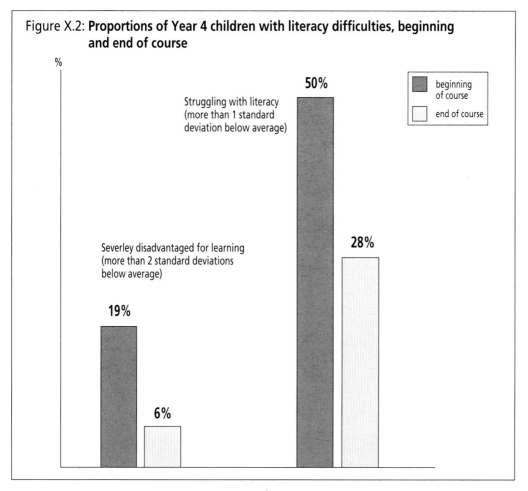

Figure X.2: **Proportions of Year 4 children with literacy difficulties, beginning and end of course**

- Many of the parents planned to go on further courses, and some had gained employment.

- Some had become more involved with their children's schools.

- The children made substantial progress in writing and in literacy generally – the (strong) effect size of 0.58 represented about 14 months' gain in reading age in three months. The proportion who were struggling with literacy went down from 50 per cent to 28 per cent, while the proportion who were severely disadvantaged for learning went down from 19 per cent to 6 per cent.

- Boys and girls made approximately equal gains

- The gains for parents were very similar to those in the Demonstration Programmes, and the gains for children were directly comparable.

## Material factors in the two models' success

The material factors which were cited by the tutors as contributing to the Programmes' success included premises, the support of the host school and its senior management and staff, effective recruitment, good attendance and retention, time for planning and evaluation, accreditation, and resources.

## Human factors in the two models' success

- The calibre of the Programme staff – in particular, their close cooperation and joint planning.

- The quality of the teaching offered – it was imaginative and attractive.

- What the parents themselves brought to the Programmes – especially commitment and support.

- What the children brought – eagerness and enthusiasm.

- The joint session – which, as in the Demonstration Programmes, was the motor of the courses' success because of the opportunities it provided for parents and children to work together in a productive and (for some) unfamiliar manner.

## Possible barriers to success

Challenges highlighted by the course tutors related to the following:

- Relationships, especially 'inducting' the parents.

- The teaching – keeping on top of the changing demands of the work.

- Assessment and accreditation, which was sometimes felt as inappropriate and too demanding for both parents and children.
- Time constraints.
- Commitment of the schools – which need to take it on board to ensure that the success is spread.

## Conclusions from observations of teaching sessions

The courses for linguistic minority families and those with a child in Year 4 showed evidence of a range of factors which contributed to their effectiveness:

- Careful and integrated joint planning
- Clear explanation of objectives to participants
- Effective use of resources
- Good management and differentiation of learning
- Excellent learning and participation in joint sessions
- Careful record-keeping.

## Lessons

- The success of the linguistic minorities model shows that the original model can be successfully implemented with different linguistic/ethnic groups. This preventive approach is not only successful but welcomed. Success depends on taking account of bilingual issues.
- The success of the Year 4 model shows that the original model can be successfully implemented at that point in the primary age range; but these courses need even more careful ground-laying and planning than those for the younger age range, because of the greater complexity and pressure of the timetable in Year 4, and the existence of other initiatives at that point (especially the National Literacy Strategy).
- Providers need further convincing of the need for assessment, and to be provided with efficient means for doing so.
- Good personal relations are key to much of the work: in successful recruitment, in cooperation between course staff, and in collaborating with host schools.
- The key factor in staffing is the calibre of staff.
- The key factor in teaching is the joint sessions, to which good planning and teaching in the separate sessions build up.
- All these factors contribute to the educational coherence of the approach.

## Principal judgments and recommendations

- Attempts to improve the basic skills of low attainers in secondary schools should take a quite different approach – such as that already adopted by the Basic Skills Agency in its Innovative Development Projects.

- The Early Years model of family literacy should continue to be widely disseminated, including among linguistic minority families.

- The Year 4 model can be successfully implemented, with care, and could serve as an exemplar for wider dissemination in primary schools.

- The essential features of the Demonstration Programmes model need to be retained, and fidelity to that model should be emphasised as an essential element in its success. These essential features are the intensive and intergenerational nature of the courses, the separate parents' and children's sessions, and above all the joint sessions where parents put into practice what they have learnt.

## CHAPTER ONE

# Origin and aims of the Study

## 1.1 Origin

In 1993/94, the Basic Skills Agency established four Family Literacy Demonstration Programmes in areas of multiple deprivation in Cardiff, Liverpool, Norfolk and North Tyneside.

The Demonstration Programmes were provided for children aged 3 to 6 and their parents. On entry, the parents had low levels of literacy, and many of their children were severely disadvantaged for learning by low development in vocabulary and in emergent reading and writing. Parents worked on their own literacy, and learned how to extend the help they gave their children. The children were given intensive early years teaching, with a strong emphasis on writing and talk as well as reading. In joint sessions, the parents worked with their children and used the strategies they had been taught for helping them.

The NFER evaluated these Programmes in the four terms from Summer 1994 to Summer 1995. The results (Brooks *et al.*, 1996) showed that the Programmes had been highly effective in boosting the parents' literacy, the parents' ability to help their children to learn to read and write, and the children's language and literacy. All the gains made during the courses were sustained in the nine months after the courses, and the children made further progress in vocabulary, reading and writing.

In 1997, the Agency commissioned the NFER to carry out a longer-term follow-up of the families who had participated in the Demonstration Programmes. The main findings (Brooks *et al.*, 1997) were that the children had maintained their gains and had not, as in too many educational interventions, slipped back; and the parents had gone from strength to strength.

Meanwhile, the Family Literacy initiative had expanded greatly. In 1997, all 22 Local Education Authorities in Wales were implementing Family Literacy schemes on the Demonstration Programme model; most courses were English-medium, though a few were Welsh-medium. In England, more than 70 LEAs had received funding for Family Literacy courses. Most of these followed the original model, for monolingual English-speaking families with a child aged 3 to 6, but in a number of areas three alternative models were being implemented which were experimental extensions of the original:

> • *working with linguistic minority families where the parents had basic skills needs and the children were aged three to six*

> • *working with parents with basic skills needs, and their children in Year 4 (therefore in primary and middle schools)*

> • *working with parents with basic skills needs, and their children in Year 7 (therefore principally in the first year of secondary school).*

The rationale for the establishment of the new models was that there was evidence of need among the target groups, and those groups had not been covered in the Demonstration Programmes – very few linguistic minority families with a child aged between 3 and 6 were involved in the Demonstration Programmes (Brooks *et al.*, 1996, pp.4, 24) and no other age group was included then. It was recognised that the model would need to be adapted for the new groups.

In most cases, these models were delivered through courses of 10 to 12 weeks' duration during school terms, though adjustments to local circumstances were envisaged. Each course was designed for up to 10 parents and 12 children. Each course was staffed by one ABS tutor and one Family Literacy tutor. For Year 4 courses this was the usual staffing, unless there happened to be a classroom assistant available. For linguistic minority courses, there would always be an extra member of staff in the Early Years and joint sessions, in most cases a bilingual support teacher; and in another room there would be the creche with its legally required number of staff, according to numbers of children on roll.

In late 1996, the Basic Skills Agency commissioned NFER to evaluate these alternative models. This is the summary report on that evaluation.

## 1.2 Context

While the Family Literacy initiative was expanding, the wider educational landscape was also changing. The previous government and the present one put great emphasis on the need to raise educational attainment. This implies both preventing educational failure for children at risk, and providing chances for those already slipping behind to catch up. The original Demonstration Programmes model and the linguistic minorities model evaluated in this study fall into the former category, while the Year 4 and Year 7 models fall into the latter. The principal educational innovation at national level in England in the period when this study was being conducted was the National Literacy Project. This precursor of the National Literacy Strategy (which succeeded it in September 1998) began in September 1996 in 15 LEAs, and was implemented across the full primary age range, Years 1 to 6. In Year 4, therefore, it overlapped with

Family Literacy, and it was in fact operating alongside Family Literacy in one or two of the schools involved in this study.

Also, by 1998 *all* LEAs in England were funded through the Standards Fund to run Family Literacy courses.

## 1.3 Aim

The aim of the evaluation was to investigate the effectiveness of the alternative models of family literacy in boosting the participating parents' and children's literacy.

## 1.4 Purpose and structure of this report

The purpose of this report is to answer two questions:

> • *What evidence is there that the Family Literacy approach can be successfully adapted for the three new groups of families?*

> • *What evidence is there that the adapted approaches are effective?*

The structure of the report is that

- – Chapter 2 outlines the approach taken (a full description of how the study was carried out is given in the Appendix). Chapter 2 and the Appendix also explain briefly why the Year 7 Model was largely unsuccessful;
- – then the findings for the Linguistic Minorities and Year 4 Models are given, in that order. For each Model, the findings are given in three chapters, covering respectively
  - □ a description of the Model
  - □ the characteristics of the participating families, and
  - □ the quantitative findings.

  These chapters are numbered 3-5 for Linguistic Minorities and 6-8 for Year 4. Conclusions about the two Models are stated at the end of chapters 5 and 8 respectively.
- – factors making for, and barriers to, the success of these models are analysed in chapter 9
- – chapter 10 states the evidence gleaned from observations of teaching sessions
- – finally, chapter 11 states the overall conclusions.

Throughout this report, any result for which statistical significance is claimed was significant at least at the 5 per cent level ($p < 0.05$); that is, the result would be likely to occur by chance only five times in every hundred.

## CHAPTER TWO

# Outline of the evaluation

─────────

(A full description of how the evaluation was carried out is given in the Appendix.)

## 2.1 Forms of information

The forms of information gathered by NFER in this study were as shown in Table 2.1.

Table 2.1: **Forms of information gathered**

| Quantitative data | | Qualitative data |
|---|---|---|
| on parents: | background information<br>literacy attainment | interviews with Adult Basic Skills (ABS) tutors and with teachers (Early Years, Year 4 or Year 7, according to Model) |
| on children: | background information<br>reading attainment<br>writing attainment | observations of teaching sessions |

## 2.2 Frequency of quantitative data collection

Background information on parents and children was gathered once, near the beginning of the course, in the Spring, Summer and Autumn terms of 1997 and the Spring term of 1998. All the other forms of quantitative data were gathered both near the beginning and just before the end of the course.

## 2.3 Quantitative data-collection instruments

Background information on participants was collected through Adult and Child Profile forms.

Estimates of the parents' literacy attainments were gathered through one of the Agency's own instruments, namely *Assessing Progress in Basic Skills: Literacy* (Basic Skills Agency, 1997). This instrument was administered by the ABS tutors, who sent the results to NFER.

Information on children's reading and writing attainment was gathered for NFER by their Family Literacy teachers.

## Linguistic minority children

To assess the overall early literacy attainment of linguistic minority children the test used was the *Literacy Baseline* within the *Reading Progress Tests* (Vincent, Crumpler and de la Mare, 1996). This test covers a suitable range of emerging and early literacy skills, and is standardised for the age range 5:00-6:04. At the discretion of their teachers, children who were thought to be too young to be assessed on this test were not given it. Raw scores were available for all the children who were given the test, but standardised scores could be calculated only for those whose ages were within the range of the norms at both the beginning and the end of the course (that is, those who were aged between 5:00 and 6:01 at the beginning). Both raw and standardised scores are reported in Chapter 5.

In addition, the Early Years teachers of linguistic minority children were asked to gather writing samples from them both at the beginning and at the end of the course, in the same way as in the original evaluation. The objective was to elicit at each stage the most advanced form of emergent or early writing which the child could produce *independently*. The instructions for this were included in the book (Gorman and Brooks, 1996) which arose from the original evaluation. The Early Years teachers were also sent further guidance notes (Gorman, 1996) expanding the analysis in Gorman and Brooks (1996).

## Children in Years 4 and 7

For children in Years 4 and 7 the main tests used were *Progress in English 9* and *Progress in English 12* (Kispal, Hagues and Ruddock, 1994) respectively. These are standardised group tests, and each covers not only reading but also other aspects of literacy, such as spelling. In particular, each level incorporates suggestions for writing tasks (though scores on these are not counted into the calculation of the standardised scores). The Family Literacy teachers were asked to set their pupils one of the writing tasks in the appropriate level of *Progress in English,* and then to impression-mark their pupils' scripts on a rising 7-point scale (1 = low, 4 = midpoint, 7 = high). The teachers were sent guidance on this, and this guidance in turn referred to the notes in the *Progress in English Teacher's Guides.*

## 2.4  Quantitative data collected

The numbers of LEAs, courses, parents and children providing quantitative data were as shown in Table 2.2.

Table 2.2:  **Numbers of LEAs, courses, parents and children providing quantitative data, by Model and overall**

| | Model | | | Total |
|---|---|---|---|---|
| | Linguistic minorities | Year 4 | Year 7 | |
| LEAs | 7 | 7 | 6 | 18* |
| Courses | 22 | 17 | 8 | 47 |
| Parents | | | | |
| – profiles | 166 | 142 | 41 | 349 |
| – tested at beginning & end | 163 | 115 | 9 | 287 |
| Children | | | | |
| – profiles | 160 | 126 | 30 | 316 |
| – tested at beginning & end | 170 | 147 | 27 | 344 |

\* Because two LEAs provided data on two Models, the total number of LEAs providing data was not 20 but 18.

The figure for linguistic minority children tested is the number who were given the writing task. The numbers tested on the Literacy Baseline were smaller, because some of the youngest children in the study were not given this test.

Table 2.2 shows that the amount of data collected on linguistic minority and Year 4 courses was adequate. However, the amount collected on Year 7 courses was very small – this is discussed in section 2.6 below.

## 2.5  Qualitative data

Qualitative data were gathered in each of the four terms. A total of 15 fieldwork visits were conducted by four NFER researchers, who on each visit interviewed the ABS tutor and the Family Literacy teacher and observed three teaching sessions (one parents-only, one children-only, and one joint). The interviews covered recruitment, teaching (both approach and content), the staff's opinions of the effectiveness of the courses, relationships with 'host' schools (including any feedback on Family Literacy children), the Agency's model of family literacy, and benefits to parents and children. For staff on linguistic minority courses only, the schedule included several specific questions on bilingual issues.

## 2.6  Comment on the Year 7 courses

As shown in Table 2.2, the amount of quantitative data gathered on Year 7 courses was very small. This was mainly because rather few such courses were actually run. From both the fieldwork evidence and course reports supplied by the LEAs it is also clear that parents' attendance on Year 7 courses was low. The paucity of quantitative data meant that there was no evidence that the Year 7 model was effective.

From the observations carried out of Year 7 courses, a number of factors seem to have meant that the Demonstration Programmes model did not adapt well to work with families with a child in Year 7. Secondary schools are much larger institutions than primary schools, with concomitantly greater problems of liaison and communication. One of the factors which contribute to the success of Family Literacy courses based in primary schools is their nearness to pupils' homes — parents do not have to travel to the courses, since the schools are almost always within walking distance. Secondary school pupils are also much more resistant to the idea of having their parents in school at all, let alone their parents being expected to attend a course with their child for several hours a week. Add to this the fact that several of the Year 7 courses which did run seem to have targeted the pupils with most severe remedial needs, who were also the most seriously disaffected pupils, and the prospects were poor.

We concluded that **the attempt to adapt the original Family Literacy model for families with a child in Year 7 was largely unsuccessful.**

We therefore recommend that **attempts to boost the basic skills of low attainers in secondary schools should take a very different approach.**

The rest of this report will focus on the linguistic minority and Year 4 models, which were successful.

## CHAPTER THREE

# Adapting the family literacy model for linguistic minority families

―――――

## 3.1 General

The overall intent of these courses was identical to that of the Demonstration Programmes: to boost the parents' and children's literacy, and the parents' ability to help their children. So for the parents, the emphasis was mainly on helping them to gain an understanding of what went on in schools, and how children actually learn, and the focus was on activities which they could do with their children and which could then be extended within the home. The main emphasis in the children's sessions was on spoken English and literacy, often through hands-on activities that the children were interested in doing. And in the joint sessions the emphasis was on encouraging natural interaction between the parents and their children, and activities were geared towards motivating the parents and children to work together on joint tasks. Much of the approach and content was therefore similar to the Demonstration Programmes, and this chapter concentrates on the adaptations made for linguistic minority families.

## 3.2 Adapting the parents' sessions

One of the most important issues raised here by course tutors was the need to ensure that course topics and materials were relevant. Tutors tried to bring in experiences or knowledge from the parents' own cultures; thus, story telling would involve tales from other countries, using published bilingual books which the parents could then use in both languages with their children. An ABS tutor in one LEA had used an Aesop fable which was well known in both Pakistan and Arabic-speaking countries, as well as in Western cultures. Often, when parents were involved in making books for their own children, these too would be made bilingual. It was very important to bring in cultural comparisons, and for tutors to have an understanding of the significance of religious festivals such as Ramadan and Eid.

An Early Years tutor in one LEA pointed out that parents on the courses might not be as familiar with British culture as a monolingual group. Consequently, a cultural item would then have to be explained before the language around it could be explored. This might be particularly true if the parents were Muslim women who did not often get out of the house, or for whom it was inappropriate to be out on their own very much. As an example of how to circumvent this problem, the tutor described a successful 'environmental print' session where the group had gone out in the local area to look at signs. The tutors had found they had to explain certain signs in ways they would not have had to use with a monolingual group.

One ABS tutor mentioned how useful it had been having a bilingual assistant working with the parents. Whilst recognising the benefit of this, the ABS tutor on another course with an Arabic-speaking parent whose English was not as well developed as that of other course members felt that, because she was used to dealing with beginners, she could usually manage to get her message across in the teaching. She would, however, set up an interpreter to telephone the parent concerned, if she needed to convey a particularly important message. *'You can't always have interpreters there so you just develop strategies for doing things ...'*

Levels of English varied considerably from group to group and so course materials had to be adapted accordingly. For example, the ABS tutor just mentioned had found that the parents on that course had a much higher level of fluency in spoken English than those on the previous course they had run. Most of the current parents were bilingual and had been through this country's education system. Therefore, although the main focus of the course had remained the same, the format had been modified slightly to allow for the higher level of English. An ABS tutor in another LEA commented that, even with support staff on hand, differences in ability could lead to problems with differentiation, and thus with pace and progress.

## 3.3 Adapting the children's sessions

Course tutors referred to the need to keep the teaching interesting for the children, with lots of opportunities for talking and listening. In one LEA, the Early Years tutor specifically mentioned the importance of ensuring that the work instilled confidence in the children. She remarked, *'... they definitely feel they are at the bottom of the heap.'* In another LEA, both tutors commented on the difficulty of coping with such a wide age range. The course they were running involved children from Reception up to Year 3, so differentiating the work effectively was often quite a challenge. As a result, the children were placed in two groups to take account of the varying levels of literacy. The Early Years tutor felt that being a teacher in the host school, which had a high proportion of children from linguistic minority families on roll, was an advantage. She commented, *'... we know all the children have language needs so we just do it anyway.'* Another Early Years tutor pointed out that writing could sometimes pose a problem, as starting points on the page differed between languages. She tended to use the languages of the parents on the course as examples.

## 3.4  Adapting the joint sessions

An important issue raised by course tutors was the need to emphasise activities at which the parents could shine. The ABS tutor in one LEA advocated this approach in courses for linguistic minority families, as a means of providing the parents with the opportunity to demonstrate their expertise, to children who might well feel linguistically or culturally superior to their parents. On this particular course, they had made family books containing recipes which the parents had brought in, and had then cooked some of the food. The school was going to publish the recipes for other parents.

Tutors referred to the need to make the sessions enjoyable, with a balance of formal and informal work. Thus, on several of the courses, tutors had developed fun activities which could then develop literacy, such as craft sessions, shopping and recipe activities, walks, etc. Although speaking English in the joint sessions was encouraged, there was evidence that parents used their first language with their children when necessary, so that the children would know what to do. As one ABS tutor pointed out, not all parents would have been able to explain fully in English, nor would all of their children have understood. Using their first language in this way avoided any breakdown in communication. At the same time, the ABS tutor could reinforce instructions in English so that the language was constantly being developed. Planned and appropriate use of bilingual assistants was also acknowledged as effective in such situations.

## CHAPTER FOUR

# Characteristics of the linguistic minority families

Between them, the seven relevant LEAs returned 166 parent profiles and 160 child profiles.

## 4.1 Languages and literacies

Not quite all of those on whom data were gathered in this Model were members of linguistic minorities: 13 parents (8 per cent) and nine children (6 per cent) were monolingual native speakers of English. Because the numbers of native speakers of English were small, and the focus of this Model was on linguistic minorities, the data from native speakers of English were excluded from the results reported in this chapter. The reporting base for this chapter is therefore 153 parents and 151 children. (The larger numbers in Chapter 5 reflect the fact that test data were returned for more parents and children than those for whom profiles were returned.)

The languages other than English spoken by the participants were as shown in Table 4.1.

Table 4.1:  **Linguistic background of participants in courses for linguistic minority families**

|  | Parents | Children |
|---|---|---|
| Bengali | 13 | 13 |
| Gujerati | 6 | 8 |
| Pashto | 2 | 2 |
| Punjabi | 103 | 100 |
| Urdu | 107 | 47 |
| Tamil | 3 | 3 |
| Farsi | 1 | 2 |
| Arabic | 7 | 6 |
| French | 1 | 1 |
| German | 1 | 0 |
| Yoruba | 1 | 0 |

The parents in particular had the chance to declare more than one language, and a substantial proportion of those declaring Punjabi and Urdu declared both. (The lower number of children with both languages declared is perhaps a function of whether or not a particular course had a bilingual member of staff who would know that many people of Pakistani origin speak both.) The numbers therefore total to more than the number of participants, and for this reason neither totals nor percentages are shown.

About 120 of the 153 parents said they understood or spoke English, but only 89 said they were literate in English. About the same number said they were literate in their first language, and 35 said they were literate in another language (different from their first language and English). The range of fluency in English, and of literacy in whichever language(s), was therefore very wide.

A total of 56 of the children were said to have had experience of writing systems other than the Roman alphabet, mainly Arabic script (whether encountered in the Koran or as used to write Urdu and the Pakistani dialect of Punjabi).

## 4.2 Gender and ethnicity

All but two (one per cent) of the parents were mothers. Of the children, 79 were girls and 72 were boys.

The ethnic origins of the parents and children were as shown in Table 4.2.

Table 4.2: **Ethnic origins of parents and children in courses for linguistic minority families**

| | Parents | | Children | |
|---|---|---|---|---|
| **Ethnic origin** | **N** | **%** | **N** | **%** |
| White | 1 | 1 | 1 | 1 |
| Indian | 6 | 4 | 8 | 5 |
| Pakistani | 120 | 78 | 110 | 73 |
| Bangladeshi | 14 | 9 | 12 | 8 |
| Other | 10 | 7 | 9 | 6 |
| Not stated | 2 | 1 | 13 | 9 |
| Total | 153 | 100 | 151 | 100 |

The one family declaring white ethnicity had French as their first language. The very high proportion of participants of Pakistani ethnicity suggests that providers had targeted areas with large numbers of Muslim families, where perhaps the women had fewer opportunities for activity outside the home, and some perhaps also had less fluency in English as a result.

## 4.3 Ages

The age-distribution of the linguistic minority parents is shown in Table 4.3.

Table 4.3: **Age-distribution of participating linguistic minority parents at start of course**

| Age | Number | % |
|---|---|---|
| under 20 | 2 | 1 |
| 20-24 | 13 | 10 |
| 25-29 | 37 | 28 |
| 30-34 | 51 | 38 |
| 35-39 | 18 | 13 |
| 40-44 | 8 | 6 |
| 45 and over | 5 | 4 |
| Total | 134 | 100 |

No information was provided on the remaining 19 parents. The great majority (79 per cent) of parents were aged between 25 and 39. The average age appeared to be somewhat older than in the Demonstration Programmes. The age-distribution of the children for whom profiles were returned was as shown in Table 4.4.

Table 4.4: **Age-distribution of participating linguistic minority children at start of course**

| Age | Number | % |
|---|---|---|
| 3 | 9 | 6 |
| 4 | 47 | 32 |
| 5 | 52 | 35 |
| 6 | 26 | 18 |
| 7 | 9 | 6 |
| 8 | 4 | 3 |
| Total | 147 | 100 |

(No information was provided on the remaining four children.)

As was the case for the parents, the children's average age appeared to be somewhat older than in the Demonstration Programmes.

## 4.4 Parents' occupations

Participating parents were asked to classify their current occupation in one of nine categories. The categories, and the distribution of responses, were as shown in Table 4.5.

Table 4.5:  **Occupations of parents on courses for linguistic minority families**

| Category | Number | % |
|---|---|---|
| Full-time employee | 0 | 0 |
| Part-time employee | 2 | 1 |
| Full-time self-employed | 1 | 1 |
| Part-time self-employed | 1 | 1 |
| In full-time education | 1 | 1 |
| Unemployed | 6 | 4 |
| Temporarily sick/disabled | 1 | 1 |
| Permanently sick/disabled | 1 | 1 |
| Looking after home/family | 128 | 90 |
| Other | 2 | 1 |
| Total | 143 | 100 |

(No information was provided for the remaining 10 parents.)

It was not clear how the one participant who said she was in full-time education was able to attend the family literacy course.

The overwhelming predominance of 'looking after home/family' in Table 4.5 reinforces the impression that most of these parents had a restricted range of activities outside the home.

## 4.5  Parents' qualifications

The parents' highest qualifications were classified in five categories ranging from 'below CSE/GCSE' to 'Higher education', and the distribution was as shown in Table 4.6.

Table 4.6:  **Highest qualification of parents on courses for linguistic minority families**

| Category | Number | % |
|---|---|---|
| none | 94 | 61 |
| CSE/GCSE | 15 | 10 |
| O-Level | 15 | 10 |
| A-Level/further education | 15 | 10 |
| higher education | 14 | 9 |
| Total | 153 | 100 |

Some of the categorisation involved finding equivalents for overseas qualifications, for example 'Pakistan secondary leaver'. The great majority of those classified as having qualifications at CSE or GCSE level had one or two passes, at low grades. Their level of qualification was barely above that of those reporting no qualifications at all. The proportion declaring themselves to have no (paper) qualifications was unusually high; but there was also a higher proportion here than is usual in Family Literacy groups of people with higher education qualifications, mostly overseas degrees. A relatively high proportion of these parents had received basic skills tuition before: 41 (27 per cent).

There was therefore a greater range than usual in Family Literacy courses in terms of linguistic fluency, literacy and qualifications. However, in general the participating linguistic minority parents were poorly qualified and not employed outside the home, and the Programmes were by design located in low-income, working-class areas with high proportions of linguistic minority families. Since this was largely the target group the Agency had in mind, *these courses had been very successful in their recruitment policy.*

## 4.6 Recruitment

In the Demonstration Programmes, personal contact was the key component of successful recruitment. This was equally true of the six courses for linguistic minority families which were visited during the evaluation. Programme staff were involved in putting up posters in the community, and in sending out leaflets and letters inviting people in to meetings in the guise of workshops or coffee mornings. In one of the LEAs, the headteacher spoke to a group of parents about the initiative. A great deal of talking to parents was done, both at meetings and out in the community, and the importance of this was underlined by tutors. An ABS tutor in one LEA said:

> '. . . the recruitment is done very much face to face, talking and showing what the last course did. We had someone come in from the last course who came and said how much she'd enjoyed it'.

This was echoed by an Early Years tutor in another LEA who commented that they '. . . *recruited through negotiation and discussion*'. In two of the LEAs this was made easier because of the previous experience Programme staff had of making contacts in the area.

The crucial role played by outreach workers who could converse with parents in their first language was specifically mentioned in four of the LEAs. The ABS tutor in one remarked:

> '. . . the school liaison person has a very strong relationship with the community, . . . knows all the mothers, I think she's wonderful'.

The Early Years tutor in the same LEA confirmed the contribution of this worker by explaining how they were able to 'tap into' the relationship she already had with parents in the community:

> *'Having the home/school officer involved in the recruitment made a big difference . . . It's important to have someone who has that rapport or relationship before you start. Her involvement was a major contribution'.*

Programme staff acknowledged the importance of using the parents' own language in the recruitment process, both through the use of outreach workers and through the recruitment material sent out. *'We do use first language for recruitment so people understand what it is they're coming to'.*

A major issue in the recruitment of linguistic minority families onto the courses was felt to be the inherent cultural restrictions and the reserved nature of the target population. Here, the vital contribution of an outreach worker who was familiar, not only with the language but also with the culture and social circumstances of the families, was recognised once more. One Early Years tutor commented that they had deliberately made their course for women only, because it would have been inappropriate for it to be mixed. She did go on to say, though, that she felt it might have been good to have some members of the white community in the group as well. However, she felt that the disadvantages, in terms of cultural differences, would have made things difficult, in particular in ensuring the relevance of topics and materials for the course.

In summary, the recruitment process for the linguistic minority courses was focused very much on the personal-contact approach, in many cases through the use of an outreach worker, yet, at the same time, was tailored towards the particular linguistic and social circumstances of the parents being targeted.

## 4.7  Retention and attendance

The six LEAs which provided quantitative data also provided, between them, course reports on 14 courses for linguistic minority families. From these it was possible to calculate average attendance and retention rates. Retention rate here is defined as the proportion of parents who were still attending at the end of the course. These rates are shown in Table 4.7. Also shown in that Table are the numbers of parents and children who were tested at the beginning and end of the course, together with the retention rate defined as the number of participants tested at the end expressed as a percentage of those tested at the beginning. These data are based on 22 courses.

Table 4.7: **Attendance and retention rates on courses for linguistic minority families**

|  | Parents | Children |
|---|---|---|
| Numbers of participants logged in course reports | 134 | 134 |
| Average attendance rate calculated from course reports | 75% | 89% |
| Average retention rate calculated from course reports | 71% | 79% |
| Number tested at beginning of course | 224 | 197 |
| Number tested at end of course | 168 | 170 |
| Average retention rate calculated from numbers tested | 75% | 86% |

Though they are based on different samples and assumptions, the two sets of retention rates are sufficiently similar to suggest that they are reasonably accurate.

In the Demonstration Programmes, attendance and retention rates for both parents and children were over 90 per cent both on average and for each of the four Programmes. The lower rates here may reflect particular circumstances in some of the participating LEAs, but also the more devolved nature and control of the new courses. However, it will be shown at the beginning of the next chapter that most of the parents who dropped out of linguistic minority courses had reasonable literacy levels to begin with.

## CHAPTER FIVE

# The benefits for linguistic minority parents and children

## 5.1 The progress in literacy made by linguistic minority parents

Data were returned for 223 parents for the beginning of the course, and for 163 at the end. The distributions of scores for the two occasions are shown in Table 5.1. For the beginning of the course, two distributions are shown: one for all those who were assessed then, the other just for those who were also assessed at the end ('returners'). Level D is the top of the relevant scale. Figure 5.1 shows the data for returners graphically.

Table 5.1: **Distribution of linguistic minority parents' literacy scores**

|  | Beginning of course | | | | End of course | |
|---|---|---|---|---|---|---|
|  | all participants | | returners | | | |
| Level | N | % | N | % | N | % |
| D | 46 | 21 | 28 | 17 | 45 | 28 |
| C | 49 | 22 | 38 | 23 | 26 | 16 |
| B | 34 | 15 | 24 | 15 | 32 | 20 |
| A | 61 | 27 | 45 | 28 | 34 | 21 |
| below A | 33 | 15 | 28 | 17 | 26 | 16 |
| Total | 223 | 100 | 163 | 100 | 163 | 100 |
| Average score (s.d.) | 2.1 (1.4) | | 2.0 (1.4) | | 2.2 (1.5) | |

Key: N = sample size; s.d. = standard deviation

The average scores (and standard deviations) shown in Table 5.1 were calculated by ascribing numerical values to the levels, as follows: below level A – 0; then levels A to D – 1 to 4. In all three cases, the 'average' was at the lower end of level B. Both these averages and the distributions of scores show that quite a few of the participating parents already had basic literacy skills, though there were still some who had low or very low skills.

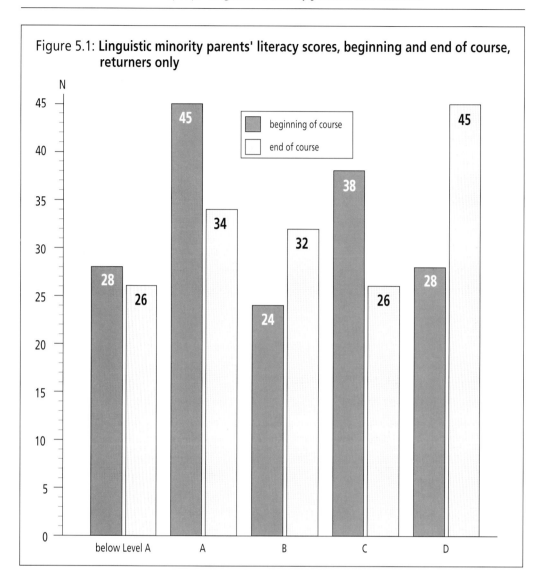

Figure 5.1: **Linguistic minority parents' literacy scores, beginning and end of course, returners only**

Comparing the two distributions for the beginning of the course shows that those who did not return for assessment at the end were predominantly at the top of the scale at the start: the proportion of parents at level D was 21 per cent of all those who started a course, but 17 per cent of returners. In a sense, therefore, most attrition or 'drop out' was among those who least needed to be on the course.

For statistical purposes, the proper comparison is between the second and third average scores in Table 5.1 – and the difference between those average scores was statistically significant, despite the shortness of the assessment scale and the apparent smallness of the absolute difference. That difference was, however, 10 per cent of the starting level, and very similar to the improvement made by parents on the Demonstration Programmes (Brooks *et al.*, 1996, 69-71). Thus many of the linguistic minority parents who stayed with the courses made significant progress in literacy in English. Parents who were below level A at the beginning were apparently an exception to this, however: the number at this level hardly changed.

No general assessment was carried out of the parents' attainment or progress in spoken English, partly because such assessment is time-consuming if it is to be valid, and partly because no standard measures of adults' oral skills exist. Staff on the linguistic minority programmes did point out at the beginning of the evaluation that not assessing the oral skills of people for whom English is an additional language could underestimate their progress. Staff on those courses were therefore encouraged to carry out such assessments locally, and to report progress in spoken English to the Basic Skills Agency and NFER alongside progress in literacy. The diversity of local instruments used for this purpose meant, however, that no generalisation of results could be achieved for spoken English, and such results are not reported.

## 5.2 Tutors' views on benefits for parents

### 5.2.1 Dual aims for parents

The majority of course tutors were in agreement that the parents' own literacy skills had improved, although an adult tutor in one LEA was not sure how far the parents' written English would develop. In another LEA, the adult tutor commented that the fact that the children had started at the same level as their parents, in terms of fluency in spoken English, was useful; they could help each other. On this particular course, a contributory factor had been the fact that the parents had all started as literate in their own language. Other tutors referred to the growth in the parents' confidence as a result of doing the course; they were far more likely to come into school and talk to teachers, they had been given the push they needed to go on to do other things.

Referring to the impact on the parents' ability to help their children, adult tutors in two LEAs commented that the course had given the parents more ideas for things to do at home and had, in effect, raised awareness of literacy and learning within the home. The adult tutor in another LEA felt that learning English through doing the course had enabled the parents to improve their relationship with their children, who often had a better command of English than they did. It had given them a sense of increased importance which had, in effect, changed the relationship between mother and child.

### 5.2.2 Parents' command of English

Tutors on the courses for linguistic minority families were all of the opinion that the parents' command of both written and spoken English had improved, although to varying degrees. Tutors reported developments in understanding texts, in reading and in simple writing tasks. One adult tutor reported that she did not think that working towards Wordpower had been very effective; the parents had not been particularly interested in the activities. However, she had noticed definite improvements in the parents' spoken English; they were not so reliant on the bilingual assistant. Another adult tutor felt some gains had been made, but that it was impossible to identify measurable gains in such a short time.

The most significant improvement highlighted by course tutors was the increase in the parents' confidence to use English; they now felt able to do more, go out into the community, and interact with people. One Early Years tutor commented on the fact that the parents often had all sorts of skills but, because they could not communicate, they often felt robbed of those skills:

> *'You can't tell someone you've got a Ph.D. because you don't know how to say it, so you can feel quite devalued as a person, because part of what you were is not part of you, because you can't tell anybody about it.'*

## 5.3  Parents' plans

### 5.3.1 Current courses

Staff were asked two questions about any plans the parents had made for after the course. The first question concerned parents on the current course (see this section); the second asked about parents on previous courses, and respondents were therefore able to refer also to how those plans had worked out.

Tutors on the courses for linguistic minority families felt that they had provided parents with a focus, and that the courses had acted as a crucial starting point for the development of future plans. Tutors observed that many of the parents were making plans as a result of attending the course. Parents' plans included attending further courses and carrying out voluntary work within school, and a couple of women were hoping to take up employment in the future. The types of courses parents were hoping to enrol on reflected a huge range of ability. This range of ability had perhaps been masked by their lack of fluency in English. The courses which parents hoped to attend ranged from ABS courses, through a nursery nurse course at college, to GCSEs.

Many of the parents' plans continued to focus on the school environment, suggesting that contact between the parents, children and the school would be maintained and hopefully developed. Parents were continuing to develop their skills; for example, in one LEA five of the eight parents on the course were going to continue with their computing and word processing by following another course at the same site.

Another parent on the course was hoping to use her bilingual skills and had applied for a vacancy as a language assistant. Within another LEA two parents were going to offer to help in the school as unpaid classroom assistants. The researcher noted the headteacher's willingness for them to do this as it might encourage others to do the same. Thus the courses not only helped parents develop and become aware of their skills, but also helped the schools become aware of parents' skills and talents, and use them. For example, in one school parents on the course had written a recipe book which was to be published by the school.

School was seen by the parents as a safe and culturally permissible environment in which to learn and to carry on learning. As an Early Years tutor observed, *'They all want to carry on if there's a chance of another course running here'*. Concern was expressed by one adult tutor that some of the parents might find it a lot more difficult taking up a course out of that safe environment.

## 5.3.2 Previous courses

Tutors were asked what parents from previous courses had gone on to do. Four of the six LEAs visited had not previously run family literacy courses. Within both the other LEAs the majority of students had gone on to do other courses and a few had gone into employment. In one, out of 14 parents on the initial course, two had gone onto an ESL course, one an RSA CLAIT course, one a bilingual skills certificate, and another was training to be a bilingual assistant in school. Two parents who had dropped out rejoined the next course and planned to go on to an ESL course. Three were doing nothing else due to family commitments, and four had left the country. In the other LEA that had run previous courses the adult tutor observed that most students had gone on to do another English course, two were in part-time employment and one was at college studying child care.

## 5.4  Parents' involvement with school

Tutors were all of the opinion that parents on the courses for linguistic minority families had become more involved with the school since attending the course. They noted that parents' contact and involvement with school had increased considerably, and tutors in one LEA commented that the parents had become more *'rooted'* in the school and were *'asked to do things more.'* The final comment reflects the fact that parental involvement is a two-way process. Not only do parents need to be aware of the skills they can offer and the contribution they can make to the school, but the school also has to be aware of what parents can offer the school and show parents that they value their skills.

An Early Years tutor in one LEA said that attending the course had, for some Asian mothers, been the first time they had actually come into school and had an opportunity to find out what went on there. She saw this as a step forward, albeit a small one, '... *only a little ripple, but at least it's a ripple.*' This tutor had been at the host school some time and could fully appreciate the significance of this development. Her perception was endorsed by the Early Years tutor in another LEA, who believed that school could be an intimidating place for many parents, but even more so for a lot of Asian parents whose experience of school was probably very different. Understanding school, and what their children do there, was '*a big plus'* for them.

Tutors observed that the courses had helped parents become more aware of what was happening in school and what their children were doing there; they now asked about their children's progress. Parents' confidence appeared to have improved since attending the course and was reflected in their becoming actively involved in projects within school, such as working on reading schemes. In one LEA, two parents who had been on the course now helped in the classroom, and others were involved in the games library, while another had begun teaching Urdu in the school. Tutors observed that parents appeared more comfortable in school and were talking to teachers more, asking them about their children's progress, which they would not have done before.

## 5.5 The progress in literacy made by linguistic minority children

Data were returned for 197 children for writing and for 166 children for the *Literacy Baseline* for the beginning of the course, and for 170 for writing and for 153 for the *Baseline* at the end. (Children whose teachers thought they were too young to be assessed on the *Baseline* were not given this test.) The distributions of scores for the two occasions are shown in Table 5.2. As for the parents, two distributions are shown for the beginning of the course. The maximum raw score on the *Baseline* is 40. Figures 5.2 and 5.3 present the returners' data for writing and *Baseline* graphically.

The increases in average scores for returners were statistically significant for both writing and the *Baseline* – but since both scales are raw scores, this would be expected in any case, because the children were growing and learning during the three months of the courses. For the *Baseline,* however, it was possible to calculate standardised scores for a subsample of the children, those who were aged between 5:00 and 6:01 at the beginning of the course. There were 65 children who fell into this age range and who provided scores at both the beginning and the end of the course. Their average standardised scores are shown in Table 5.3. The gains made by boys and girls were very similar on both instruments and (in the case of *Baseline* ) in both raw and standardised scores, and did not differ significantly.

Table 5.2:  **Distribution of linguistic minority children's literacy scores**

| | Beginning of course | | | | End of course | |
| | all participants | | returners | | | |
| Score | N | % | N | % | N | % |
|---|---|---|---|---|---|---|
| *Writing* | | | | | | |
| 7 | 11 | 6 | 10 | 6 | 33 | 19 |
| 6 | 19 | 10 | 18 | 11 | 29 | 17 |
| 5 | 15 | 8 | 12 | 7 | 23 | 14 |
| 4 | 51 | 26 | 43 | 25 | 47 | 28 |
| 3 | 35 | 18 | 31 | 18 | 21 | 12 |
| 2 | 37 | 19 | 35 | 21 | 15 | 9 |
| 1 | 29 | 15 | 21 | 12 | 2 | 1 |
| Total | 197 | 100 | 170 | 100 | 170 | 100 |
| Average score (s.d.) | 3.4 (1.7) | | 3.5 (1.7) | | 4.7 (1.6) | |
| **Raw score bands** | N | % | N | % | N | % |
| *Literacy Baseline* | | | | | | |
| 35-40 | 4 | 2 | 3 | 2 | 40 | 26 |
| 30-34 | 18 | 11 | 16 | 10 | 18 | 12 |
| 25-29 | 10 | 6 | 9 | 6 | 24 | 16 |
| 20-24 | 27 | 16 | 25 | 16 | 15 | 10 |
| 15-19 | 22 | 13 | 20 | 13 | 22 | 14 |
| 10-14 | 34 | 20 | 32 | 21 | 21 | 14 |
| 5-9 | 35 | 21 | 33 | 22 | 10 | 7 |
| 0-4 | 16 | 10 | 14 | 9 | 5 | 3 |
| Total | 166 | 100 | 153 | 100 | 153 | 100 |
| Average score (s.d.) | 15.9 (9.7) | | 15.5 (9.6) | | 24.0 (10.9) | |

Key: N = sample size; s.d. = standard deviation

The gain of 10.8 standardised score points represents just over two-thirds of a standard deviation. The progress implied can be judged from the standardisation tables for the test. The average standardised score of 93.5 for these 65 children at the beginning of the course would translate into a reading age of 5:02, while their average standardised score of 104.3 at the end of the course would translate into a reading age of 5:09 – an average gain of 7 months of reading age in 3 months.

Table 5.3:  **Average standardised scores of children aged 5:00-6:01 at beginning of course (N=65)**

|  | Beginning of course | End of course |
|---|---|---|
| Average standardised score | 93.5 | 104.3 |
| (s.d.) | (16.9) | (14.8) |

Key: N = sample size; s.d. = standard deviation

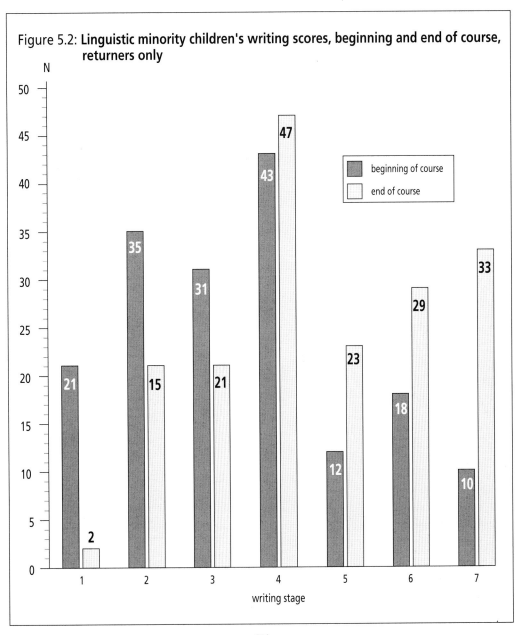

Figure 5.2: **Linguistic minority children's writing scores, beginning and end of course, returners only**

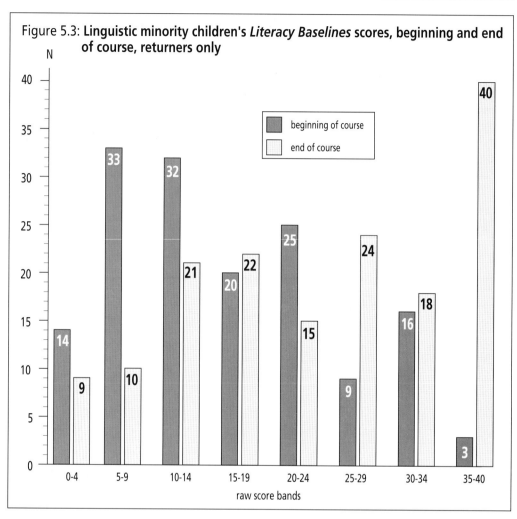

Figure 5.3: **Linguistic minority children's** *Literacy Baselines* **scores, beginning and end of course, returners only**

Because the *Literacy Baseline* provided standardised scores for this subsample, it was also possible to calculate the effect size for the progress made by these children. The formula used was

$$\frac{\text{average gain in standardised score points}}{15}$$

where the term above the line can be expanded to

(average standardised score at post-test) − (average standardised score at pre-test).

The divisor represents the standard deviation of the normal distribution. (For the rationale for using this divisor, and the whole formula, and on effect sizes in general, see Brooks *et al.*, 1998, 63-5.)

The effect size calculated in this way was 0.72, which is very powerful.

These statistically based estimates of the impact of the courses for the subsample for whom standardised scores could be calculated permit clear judgments on the increases in average raw scores for the full sample, on both instruments. In the judgment of the research team both increases were impressive.

In terms of the *Baseline*, the progress of the full sample can again be judged from the standardisation tables. The average raw score for the beginning of the course, 15.5, is the score that would be achieved by the average child of age 5:02 – but since the children in this study had an average age several months older than that, this was a distinctly low average score for this group. The average raw score for the end of the course, 24.0, is the score that would be achieved by the average child of age 5:09 – in other words, the full sample had also on average made 7 months' progress in 3 months.

In terms of writing, the full sample can be compared with the children in the Demonstration Programmes. Those children were almost all monolingual English-speakers. In terms of social circumstances other than language they were very similar to the linguistic minority children in this study (though this group was slightly older on average). The average scores for the 279 'returner' children in the Demonstration Programmes evaluation, assessed on this same scale and writing task, were 3.5 for the beginning of the course (identical to the score here), and 4.1 for the end (Brooks *et al.*, 1996, 53) *versus* 4.7 here. The gain made by children in the Demonstration Programmes was judged to be highly satisfactory, and the gain made by the children in this study was twice as large.

In the evaluation of the Demonstration Programmes (Brooks et al., 1996, 39-40, 53-54), it was also shown that, on the scale used for the assessment of young children's writing, the crucial step was from point 4 (child can write own name and some letters) to point 5 (words). Among the 170 'returners' in the present study, only 40 (24 per cent) had already made that transition at the beginning of the course; by the end, 85 (exactly 50 per cent) were at or beyond point 5. Some of these would have made that progress anyway, in the normal course of events; but it is unlikely that 26 per cent of such a group would have done so in a 12-week period. This finding therefore reinforces the picture of substantial added progress in writing.

Both in general literacy and specifically in writing, therefore, these linguistic minority children had made excellent progress.

## 5.6 Tutors' views on benefits for children

On the courses for linguistic minority families, tutors were all of the opinion that the children had made some improvements in their command of English, particularly so with spoken English. Tutor comments referred to the supportive nature of the small group sessions, and the fact that there was more opportunity than normal for the children to interact with adults. Children had gained in confidence and consequently become more fluent in the language. One Early Years tutor reported a very big improvement in two children who did not speak at all at the beginning of the course; they were now much more communicative.

## 5.7 Feedback from children's schools

The majority of tutors on the courses for linguistic minority families had received positive feedback from children's schools. Teachers' comments related to improvements in children's progress generally, increased confidence and/or greater participation in the classroom. A number of teachers had commented on specific developments with individual children, such as improvements in behaviour, communication and interaction.

## 5.8 Conclusions on courses for linguistic minority families

- The original Family Literacy model had been appropriately and successfully adapted for linguistic minority families.
- The main linguistic minority recruited was speakers of Urdu and Punjabi.
- The linguistic minority parents were in general poorly qualified and not employed outside the home.
- The recruitment policy was largely successful, and depended mainly on personal contact.
- Attendance and retention rates (89 and 86 per cent respectively) were reasonably high for the children, and quite high for the parents (75 per cent in both cases).
- The parents significantly improved their literacy in English – their average final score was 10 per cent higher than the average starting score.
- Their tutors said the parents' confidence both generally and in their command of spoken and written English had grown.
- The tutors also said the parents' ability to help their children had improved.
- Many of the parents planned to go on further courses.
- Many had become more involved with their children's schools.
- The children made substantial progress in writing and in early literacy generally – the (powerful) effect size of 0.72 represented about seven months' gain in reading age in three months, and the gain in writing was about twice as large as in the Demonstration Programmes.
- Boys and girls made approximately equal gains.
- Both their Early Years tutors and their school teachers said the children's fluency in spoken English had improved.
- **The gains for parents were very similar to those in the Demonstration Programmes, and the gains for children were slightly larger.**

28

## CHAPTER SIX

# Adapting the model for families with a child in Year 4

Adapting the original Family Literacy model for families with a child in Year 4 was mainly a matter of choosing content and activities suitable for children aged 8 to 9, and for their parents to engage in with them. However, some of the schools in this study were already implementing the Literacy Hour, because they were participating in the National Literacy Project. There is evidence that in the Autumn term of 1997 most schools were already giving at least an hour a day to literacy (Brooks and Keys, 1998). And in the Spring term of 1998 some schools were using 'literacy hours' other than the National Literacy Project's version, including some that had been developed earlier (Sainsbury, 1998). All of this meant that three sessions for literacy per week outside the Year 4 classroom had to be justified to schools even more convincingly than in the Demonstration Programmes.

## 6.1  Adapting the parents' sessions

In three of the five LEAs, ABS tutors commented on the need to boost the parents' confidence, to show them that they had skills they were perhaps not aware of, and that the things they were already doing at home with their children were of value. Thus work on the parents' skills was achieved through looking at the children's curriculum, and how the parents could become more involved in their children's education. Tutors referred to work on basic skills which could be used in everyday life, such as letter writing, dictionary skills, using indices and catalogues, word processing and communication skills.

Activities offered in the parents' sessions on the Year 4 courses included:

- discussion;
- work on spelling (rules, strategies, most commonly misspelt words);
- comprehension;
- wordsearches;
- decoding symbols;
- accessing information from charts and other reference material;

- communication skills;
- reading;
- filling in forms;
- letter writing;
- CVs;
- looking at children's games;
- making games;
- making books;
- puppet making;
- first aid;
- museum visit followed up by writing a letter of thanks;
- library visit;
- work on library referencing systems;
- talks from visiting speakers;
- preparation for the joint sessions;
- Wordpower.

Tutors reported practical activities as being particularly successful with parents. ABS tutors in two LEAs specifically mentioned games in this context, both making games for children, and playing them as adults before introducing them to the children. One of the tutors found that making the games drew attention to the parents' skills whilst, at the same time, facilitating communication within the group.

Strategies to help children with their spelling were also popular with parents, as they were able to improve their own spelling at the same time. Work on interviewing skills and CVs went down well with parents. One ABS tutor said she introduced this near the end of the course when it had begun to assume some relevance and importance for the parents:

> '...they get to write their own CV, it's theirs for when they leave..., and try and encourage them to think long term, there is a future, there is something else... another string to their bow, it gives them the opportunity to do something else with their lives, so they are very successful ones, CV writing, interview skills, preparing them perhaps for the outside world as it were. A lot of them are entrenched at home.'

Other activities perceived by tutors to be successful were first aid, a session on 'What is reading?', and trips out.

## 6.2 Adapting the children's sessions

Tutors were very conscious of the need to dovetail the Family Literacy work with the children's normal classroom programme, which in some cases included the National Literacy Project. In the case of Year 4 tutors who were not teachers in the host schools, this was achieved through close liaison with class teachers. One very important consideration for course tutors was the need to build up the children's levels of confidence and their self-esteem. One Year 4 tutor said she was concerned to enable the children to be more positive about themselves, to help them '... *to realise that they can do a lot of things that they are not very positive about'*. The hope was, that by raising levels of self-esteem and improving their literacy skills, the children would then find the other work in the classroom easier. This Year 4 tutor also commented that she tried to teach the children how to remain on task and to complete work, both important skills that could be effectively taught in a small group situation, and which would help them when back in the classroom environment. Another consideration was to show the children that learning could be fun.

On the Year 4 courses, the activities offered in the children's sessions included:

- developing basic skills, starting off at word level and moving up to sentence level, then using wider sentence connectors to create longer sentences, and finally linking sentences together;
- a balance of writing, reading, speaking and listening;
- sequencing activities;
- writing stories to pictures;
- spelling;
- playing games;
- making books;
- making jigsaws;
- making a scrapbook;
- looking at and talking about posters;
- designing posters;
- painting;
- drawing cartoons;
- book reviews;
- cooking;
- quizzes;
- word processing.

Once again, tutors found that the more practical activities such as cooking, quizzes and making things were most popular with the children. Initially, some of the tutors had found the children quite reluctant to settle down to more formal writing tasks. However, this had got easier as the course progressed, especially when the time was broken up with a variety of tasks and teaching approaches.

## 6.3 Adapting the joint sessions

The joint sessions provided an opportunity for parents to realise just what their children were capable of, and to help parents understand how to encourage the children to do things independently without interfering. Some of the parents found it difficult to relate to, and thus to communicate with, their children. Course tutors could use the joint sessions to model ways of helping the children and enable parents to step back a little, to guide the children and see, as one Year 4 tutor commented, *'... that they are capable of doing more maybe than they give them credit for.'*

An emphasis on helping parents not to interfere, or take over from the children, in joint session activities was highlighted by tutors in two LEAs. However, the ABS tutor in another LEA, which had run a Demonstration Programme, thought that the parents of Year 4 children did not need as much support in these sessions as those of younger children. She and her Year 4 colleague had been able to hand over the running of the joint sessions to the parents after outlining the task to them. For her, the joint sessions had been *'a joy'*.

Course tutors in three of the LEAs commented on the way in which they tried to ensure that sessions linked up, so that the adult session usually tied in with the joint session and was differentiated accordingly. The joint session gave the parents the chance to see how they could use the things they had learnt about how children are taught in school, to help their children and build up their confidence. As one ABS tutor remarked:

> *'It's to show parents in practical terms how you can put into practice what we have talked about, usually in the mornings. So like today when we were talking about writing and the whole range of different writing skills that children need to develop, showing them with a practical activity how you are doing some of that . . .'*

Activities offered in the joint sessions on the Year 4 courses included:

- speaking and listening activities;
- reading;

- writing;
- looking at print;
- reading labels;
- wordsearches;
- dictionary work;
- accessing information from reference material;
- communication and vocabulary work;
- cookery;
- quizzes;
- making games;
- playing games;
- making books;
- making models;
- making puppets;
- writing a script and acting out a play;
- painting;
- talks and demonstrations (with activities to do) from visiting speakers.

Year 4 course tutors felt that the interaction between parents and their children in the joint sessions had definitely improved as the course progressed. Several of them referred to things being a little difficult at first, parents and children themselves had found it rather strange, and some parents had seemed quite impatient to begin with. However, attitudes and relationships had developed positively during the weeks of the course. On the whole, tutors had found that the parents and the children enjoyed working together, one ABS tutor going as far as to say that both sides were *'desperately keen'* to do so. Another ABS tutor remarked that the improvement in the relationships had led to the parents doing more with the children at home, because they now had the necessary skills.

In two LEAs, course tutors mentioned specific cases where the interaction between parents and children had improved. In one, the ABS tutor referred to a grandfather on the course who, with his wife, was bringing up their grandson. He had found it difficult at first, as things were very different from when he was bringing up his children. The tutor felt he had gained a lot from being on the course; he could now stand back and allow his grandson to develop at his own pace. The Year 4 tutor in the other LEA remarked on improvements in the interaction amongst the group as a whole. There were some very low attaining children in the group and the more able parents all teamed up to help. At the same time, one parent had particular problems with low confidence and poor self-esteem. The other parents were extremely supportive towards her and the tutor believed, '*. . . it's sort of given the whole group a team spirit.*'

## CHAPTER SEVEN

# Characteristics of the families with a child in Year 4

Between them, the seven Year 4 LEAs returned 142 parent profiles and 126 child profiles.

## 7.1 Gender, ethnicity and language

All but nine (6 per cent) of the parents were mothers. Of the children, 65 were girls and 61 were boys.

All but 14 (10 per cent) of the parents and 14 (11 per cent) of the children were of white ethnicity; and all but 20 (14 per cent) of the parents and five (4 per cent) of the children were monolingual native speakers of English. Because of the small numbers of members of ethnic and linguistic minorities, neither of these variables is used for reporting; but the data for participants of ethnicities other than white and for non-native speakers of English are included in the general analyses.

## 7.2 Ages

The age-distribution of the Year 4 parents is shown in Table 7.1.

Table 7.1: **Age-distribution of participating parents of Year 4 children at start of course**

| Age | Number | % |
| --- | --- | --- |
| under 25 | 0 | 0 |
| 25-29 | 25 | 18 |
| 30-34 | 48 | 35 |
| 35-39 | 37 | 27 |
| 40-44 | 15 | 11 |
| 45 and over | 14 | 10 |
| Total | 139 | 100 |

No information was provided on the remaining three parents. The great majority (80 per cent) of parents were aged between 25 and 39. The absence of parents aged under 25 was consistent with the fact that the children involved were aged 8 or 9.

Since the Year 4 children were all drawn from that school year, their ages ranged between 8:00 and 9:08 at the beginning of the course (depending on the term in which it took place).

## 7.3 Parents' occupations

Participating parents were asked to classify their current occupation in one of nine categories. The categories, and the distribution of responses, were as shown in Table 7.2.

**Table 7.2: Occupations of parents of Year 4 children**

| Category | Number | % |
|---|---|---|
| Full-time employee | 8 | 6 |
| Part-time employee | 30 | 23 |
| Full-time self-employed | 0 | 0 |
| Part-time self-employed | 4 | 3 |
| In full-time education | 0 | 0 |
| Unemployed | 13 | 10 |
| Temporarily sick/disabled | 3 | 2 |
| Permanently sick/disabled | 4 | 3 |
| Looking after home/family | 67 | 50 |
| Other | 4 | 3 |
| Total | 133 | 100 |

(No information was provided for the remaining nine parents.)

It was not clear how the eight parents who declared themselves to be in full-time employment were able to attend the courses.

Almost exactly half the parents in Year 4 courses were looking after home or family, a much lower proportion than in the linguistic minorities group. Just under 30 per cent were employed (mainly part-time), while 10 per cent were unemployed.

## 7.4 Parents' qualifications

The parents' highest qualifications were classified in five categories ranging from 'below CSE/GCSE' to 'Higher education', and the distribution was as shown in Table 7.3.

Table 7.3:  **Highest qualification of parents of Year 4 children**

|  | Number | % |
|---|---|---|
| none | 74 | 52 |
| CSE/GCSE | 19 | 13 |
| O-Level | 19 | 13 |
| A-Level/further education | 26 | 18 |
| higher education | 4 | 3 |
| Total | 142 | 100 |

Again, the great majority of those classified as having qualifications at CSE or GCSE level had one or two passes, at low grades. Most of the further education qualifications were in vocational subjects. Only 21 parents (15 per cent) had received basic skills tuition before.

The participating parents were therefore in general poorly qualified and not employed outside the home, and the Programmes were by design located in low-income, working-class areas. Since this was largely the target group the Agency had in mind, **these courses had been very successful in their recruitment policy.**

## 7.5  Recruitment

The personal approach to recruitment was also applied in the five Year 4 courses visited. In one LEA, a course had already been run at the school the year before and so the parents of that course, in effect, became recruiters for the new course, passing on positive messages about what they had done. In three LEAs, staff running the Year 4 courses had been involved in the Demonstration Programmes, and so had been able to use their previous experience of the Early Years courses to devise an appropriate format for recruitment for the Year 4 courses.

Letters, leaflets or flyers about the course were sent out to parents of Year 4 children asking them to come into school and find out about the course. They were invited in to coffee mornings, meetings or workshops where parents and their children could come in and try out a range of activities together. Parents were then asked if they would like to sign up for the course.

In two of the LEAs, the Area Coordinator had been particularly involved in the recruitment process. In one, based on her experience of working in other authorities, she had initiated the making of a video of children in school on a typical day. She had found this to be a particularly successful way of getting parents, who often had little idea of what actually went on, into school.

In another LEA, the Area Coordinator had identified schools which were already part of the (then) National Literacy Project, and had gone in to talk to the headteacher about also becoming involved in Family Literacy. She then spoke to Year 4 teachers, together with the rest of the staff, at a staff meeting, so that the whole staff was aware of what was going on. She and the Programme staff wanted the Family Literacy course to be seen by the Year 4 teachers in school as complementary to what they were already doing. They also thoroughly appreciated that it was a long time for Year 4 children to be out of class. It was very much a case of preparing the ground by ensuring that the headteacher and the rest of the staff were kept as fully informed as possible of what was happening, something that was underlined by both tutors in another LEA, who commented that they tried to ensure staff knew exactly *'. . . what we are about and what we are trying to do.'* After the initial preparation, the Area Coordinator in the LEA mentioned above had sent out flyers about the course to all the Year 4 parents to avoid anyone feeling upset at being targeted. Next, the teachers, along with the headteacher, had spoken to specific parents who they felt would benefit from doing the course. They had informed parents with GC(S)E qualifications that this course would perhaps not be suitable for them. They had also run 'taster' days and were planning to organise a display board, with press cuttings and evaluations from some of the parents on previous courses.

Involving the teachers in school in recruitment was specifically mentioned by course tutors in three other LEAs. In two, the Year 4 tutors were actually teachers in the school. They had spoken to parents at initial meetings and one had then talked to parents in her role as class teacher. And in the LEA where the Year 4 tutor was not a teacher in the host school, the importance of enlisting the help of the teachers in school, who knew the families better, was also recognised.

The Area Coordinator who had done so much initial paving of the way in schools saw the involvement of host school teachers in the recruitment process as a way of forging closer links with the school. It meant that there was less hostility towards the initiative, especially in cases where headteachers had perhaps not fully disseminated the necessary information to their staff.

A particular issue raised by course tutors was the difficulty of actually reaching Year 4 parents, many of whom no longer brought their children into school and so were no longer such a *'ready target'*. At the same time, it was felt that several parents have, by the time their children are in Year 4, *'picked up'* their lives and gone on to either part- or full-time work. As a result, some of the course tutors had found it useful to communicate with parents through the children, in the hope that they would then transmit some of their enthusiasm to their parents.

Thus, once again, effective recruitment for the Year 4 courses depended very much on personal contact, through the use of previous course members as recruiters, through talking to parents at various events in school, through the involvement of school staff who then approached parents, and through the children themselves.

## 7.6  Retention and attendance

The five LEAs which provided quantitative data also provided, between them, course reports on 14 courses for families with a child in Year 4. From these it was possible to calculate average attendance and retention rates. Retention rate here is defined as the proportion of parents who were still attending at the end of the course. These rates are shown in Table 7.4. Also shown in that Table are the numbers of parents and children who were tested at the beginning and end of the course, together with the retention rate defined as the number of participants tested at the end expressed as a percentage of those tested at the beginning. These data are based on 17 courses.

Table 7.4:  **Attendance and retention rates on courses for families with a child in Year 4**

|  | Parents | Children |
|---|---|---|
| Number of participants logged in course reports | 130 | 134 |
| Average attendance rate calculated from course reports | 87% | 92% |
| Average retention rate calculated from course reports | 83% | 94% |
| Number tested at beginning of course | 139 | 156 |
| Number tested at end of course | 115 | 147 |
| Average retention rate calculated from numbers tested | 83% | 94% |

Though they were based on different samples, the two sets of retention rates were identical – this suggests that they were reliable measures.

In the Demonstration Programmes, attendance and retention rates for both parents and children were over 90 per cent both on average and for each of the four Programmes. The rates here for children were in the same range, and those for parents were not far below.

## CHAPTER EIGHT

# The benefits for Year 4 children and their parents

## 8.1 The progress in literacy made by parents of Year 4 children

Data were returned for 139 parents for the beginning of the course, and for 115 at the end. The distributions of scores for the two occasions are shown in Table 8.1. As in chapter 5, two distributions are shown for the beginning of the course: one for all who were assessed then, the other just for returners. Figure 8.1 shows the returners' data graphically.

Table 8.1: **Distribution of literacy scores of parents of Year 4 children**

| | Beginning of course | | | | End of course | |
| | all participants | | returners | | | |
| Level | N | % | N | % | N | % |
|---|---|---|---|---|---|---|
| D | 63 | 45 | 51 | 44 | 67 | 58 |
| C | 57 | 41 | 48 | 42 | 42 | 37 |
| B | 16 | 12 | 14 | 12 | 4 | 4 |
| A | 1 | 1 | 0 | 0 | 2 | 2 |
| below A | 2 | 1 | 2 | 2 | 0 | 0 |
| Total | 139 | 100 | 115 | 100 | 115 | 100 |
| Average score (s.d.) | 3.3 (0.8) | | 3.3 (0.8) | | 3.5 (0.7) | |

Key: N = sample size; s.d. = standard deviation
Note: For how the average scores and standard deviations were calculated, see chapter 5.

Table 8.1 shows that very few parents on these courses were assessed as having very low literacy. Consistent with this, the average scores were within level C, and distinctly higher than those for the linguistic minority parents.

The difference between the returners' beginning and end of course average scores was again statistically significant, despite the shortness of the assessment scale and the apparent smallness of the absolute difference. The gain was about 6 per cent of the starting level. Thus many of the Year 4 parents who stayed with the courses made significant progress in literacy in English.

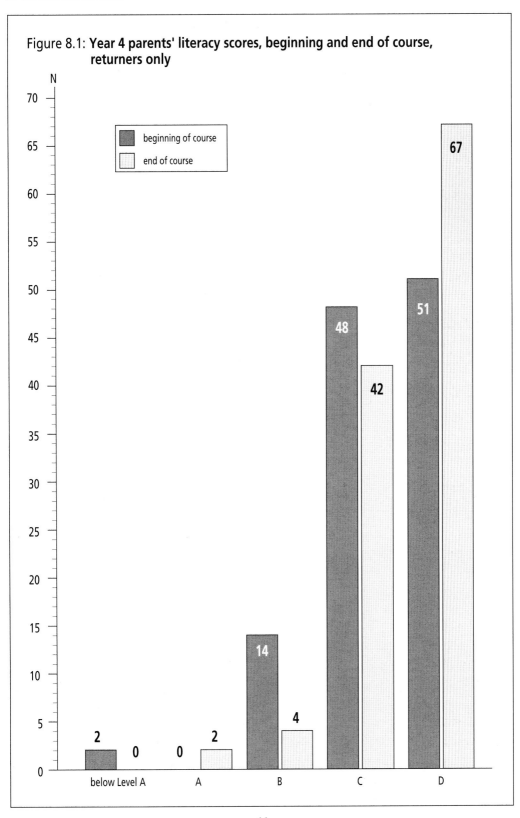

Figure 8.1: **Year 4 parents' literacy scores, beginning and end of course, returners only**

## 8.2 Tutors' views on benefits for parents

Tutors on all five Year 4 courses felt that the parents' literacy skills had improved, and they had also gained the skills necessary to be able to work with, and help, their children. One Year 4 tutor felt that the experience they had gained from being involved in the Demonstration Programmes had been helpful. She believed they had got the balance right; the parents and the children were both gaining fulfilment, and they were benefiting greatly from working together in the joint sessions.

Course tutors were in agreement that the parents' own skills had improved, one Year 4 tutor particularly mentioning the benefits to the two fathers on their course, who had had little or no involvement with school before doing the course. Tutors referred to parents' gains in confidence and being able to talk more about what they were doing with the children. A final comment came from an adult tutor in one LEA who felt that the parents were becoming accustomed to spending more time with their children.

## 8.3 Parents' plans

### 8.3.1 Current courses

Tutors on the Year 4 courses observed that parents' plans were fairly tentative and that it was too early to tell what parents were going to do. The focus of parents' plans was usually on further learning, although one adult tutor said that one or two parents had got jobs after the course. An adult tutor in another LEA commented that many of the parents were wanting to do something but they were not sure what. The adult tutors generally appeared to be acting as facilitators, providing parents with educational guidance and informing them of the learning opportunities available to them, generally outside the school environment, such as college courses and open learning. Continuity and contact was hopefully going to be maintained in two LEAs, as there were plans for parents to carry on with adults-only sessions in order to finish their certificates and word processing courses. It was interesting to note that three of the five Year 4 tutors did not know what parents' plans were.

### 8.3.2 Parents' plans – previous courses

Previous courses had been run in three of the five relevant LEAs. Tutors in these LEAs observed that parents from previous courses had usually gone on to do other courses. The courses they went on to generally had either a school- or a community-based focus, such as 'Parents as Educators' or Classroom Assistant courses or access courses in the community. In one LEA the Year 4 tutor said that 70 per cent of parents had opted for further courses where they could be accredited for supporting their children in the classroom. In another LEA 39 per cent (11) of parents had gone on to take up ABS courses.

A number of parents had entered employment, whilst others had been involved in a 'community shop' and a 'community flat' which had also led to the development of other courses. Those parents who had entered employment were generally in part-time jobs; for example, one woman had become a dinner supervisor. Although the job might be seen as quite 'minor', in terms of individual progression it was a 'major' development. Tutors also highlighted specific 'success stories', such as one woman who had gone on to take a business and accountancy course and was hoping to become an accountant. Another woman who, when she started the course, had been fairly negative about the school, actually became a school governor and one of its staunchest advocates.

Tutors highlighted the positive impact and effects of previous courses leading to greater confidence for the parents which, in turn, had given them the impetus to move on. As one Year 4 tutor observed:

> *'It sort of raises their confidence that they can actually do something and it sort of makes them less frightened to go on and do something formal.'*

This was reinforced by an adult tutor when she commented that *'it's just given them that little seed'*, whether to go on to do another course or to get a job. For other parents the courses had given them the much needed confidence to actually offer assistance in school. As one adult tutor observed: *'. . . for some parents just being brave enough to go and help in school is quite a big step.'*

## 8.4 Parents' involvement with school

Tutors' responses to this question highlighted variable levels of parental involvement. Furthermore, two Year 4 tutors did not feel that they could answer the question, whilst two other tutors thought that this was difficult to quantify as some parents were quite involved with the school before attending the course.

In two LEAs tutors felt that parents were more involved with the school now, but to differing degrees. For example, one Year 4 tutor commented that parents were now not as frightened to come into school to talk to teachers, and that they were also coming in to hear readers and doing more reading with their children at home. For some parents their level of involvement with school was still relatively minor, but could be seen as significant in terms of their progression since beginning the course. An adult tutor described one woman who still had very little confidence but who actually spoke to the headteacher when he visited the parents' session. The tutor commented that previously she would have relied on her daughter but now she did more for herself.

Two adult tutors commented that they did not think that parents were very involved with the school now. One observed that a lot of the parents still felt intimidated by the teachers, and the other said that when the headteacher came in to talk to the group only one parent had spoken to him before and the others were surprised how normal he was! So perhaps, after realising his 'normality', the parents may have felt a little more confident about approaching him in the future.

## 8.5  The progress in literacy made by Year 4 children

Data on writing were returned for 156 children for the beginning of the course, and for 147 for the end of the course; data were returned for *Progress in English 9* for 144 children at both stages. The distributions of scores for the two occasions are shown in Table 8.1. The writing tasks were scored impressionistically on a rising 7-point scale. Since *Progress in English 9* is a standardised test, the scores for that test are given in score ranges corresponding to standard deviations (±15 score points). Because all children tested on *Progress in English 9* at the beginning of the course were also tested at the end, there is no need to show two separate distributions for the beginning of the course in this instance. Returners' data for writing and *Progress in English* are shown graphically in Figures 8.2 and 8.3.

The differences in average scores for returners were statistically significant for both writing and *Progress in English 9*. The gains made by boys and girls were very similar on both instruments, and did not differ significantly.

Because *Progress in English 9* provides standardised scores, it is possible to compare the distribution of the scores on this test achieved by these Year 4 children to the national ('normal') distribution. In a normal distribution, 16 per cent of children (one in seven) score below 85, and can be considered to be struggling with literacy; within that group, 2.5 per cent of children (one in 40) score below 70, and can be considered severely disadvantaged for learning. In the sample of Year 4 children in this study, 50 per cent (one in two) scored below 85 (were struggling) at the beginning of the course, and 19 per cent (almost one in five) scored below 70 (were severely disadvantaged for learning). These comparisons show both that the proportions with educational problems were significantly greater than the norm, and that these children were validly targeted.

Adding the data for the end of the course to the comparison shows that a great many of these children had made good progress: the proportion who were struggling had gone down from 50 per cent to 28 per cent, while the proportion who were severely disadvantaged for learning had gone down from 19 per cent to 6 per cent. These gains are at least comparable to, perhaps slightly better than, those achieved by the much younger children in the Demonstration Programmes evaluation (see Brooks *et al.*, 1996, 50-51).

Table 8.2: **Distribution of Year 4 children's literacy scores**

| | Beginning of course | | | | End of course | |
| | all participants | | returners | | | |
| Score | N | % | N | % | N | % |
|---|---|---|---|---|---|---|
| **Writing** | | | | | | |
| 7 | 12 | 8 | 11 | 7 | 5 | 3 |
| 6 | 4 | 3 | 4 | 3 | 7 | 5 |
| 5 | 4 | 3 | 4 | 3 | 23 | 16 |
| 4 | 40 | 26 | 38 | 26 | 34 | 23 |
| 3 | 36 | 23 | 34 | 23 | 52 | 35 |
| 2 | 48 | 31 | 45 | 31 | 23 | 16 |
| 1 | 12 | 8 | 11 | 7 | 3 | 2 |
| Total | 156 | 100 | 147 | 100 | 147 | 100 |
| Average score (s.d.) | 3.2 (1.6) | | 3.2 (1.6) | | 3.6 (1.3) | |
| **Standardised score bands** | | | N | % | N | % |
| **Progress in English 9** | | | | | | |
| over 130 | | | 0 | 0 | 3 | 2 |
| 115-130 | | | 8 | 6 | 15 | 11 |
| 100-114 | | | 28 | 19 | 35 | 24 |
| 85-99 | | | 36 | 25 | 51 | 35 |
| 70-84 | | | 44 | 31 | 31 | 22 |
| Below 70 | | | 28 | 19 | 9 | 6 |
| Total | | | 144 | 100 | 144 | 100 |
| Average score (s.d.) | | | 87.1 (14.5) | | 95.8 (16.4) | |

Key: N = sample size; s.d. = standard deviation

The average standardised scores for the beginning and end of the course on *Progress in English 9* were 87.1 and 95.8 respectively. Inspection of the standardisation tables for the test showed that, for two children with the same raw score to achieve these different standardised scores, they would have to be 14 months apart in age. This suggests that these Year 4 children had achieved on average just over a year's progress in literacy in three months.

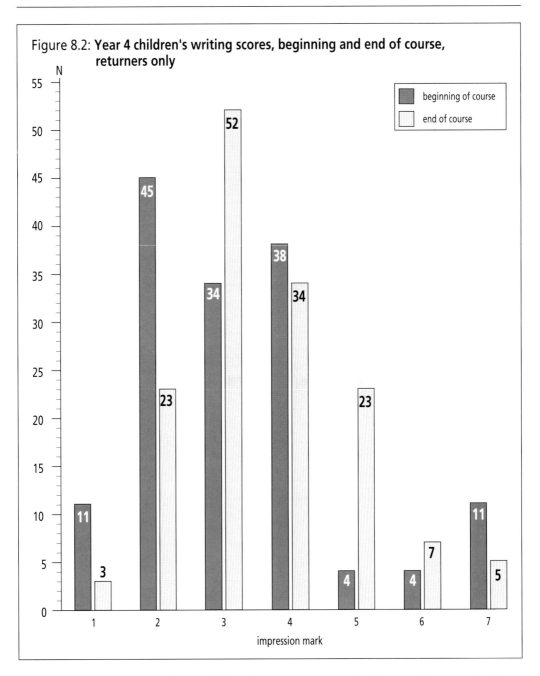

Figure 8.2: **Year 4 children's writing scores, beginning and end of course, returners only**

Because *Progress in English 9* (like the *Literacy Baseline*) provides standardised scores, it was again possible to calculate the effect size for the progress made by these children. (For the formula used, see chapter 5.)

The effect size for these children was 0.58, which is again very powerful.

The average gain in writing made by the Year 4 children was also substantial – it was 12.5 per cent of the average starting level.

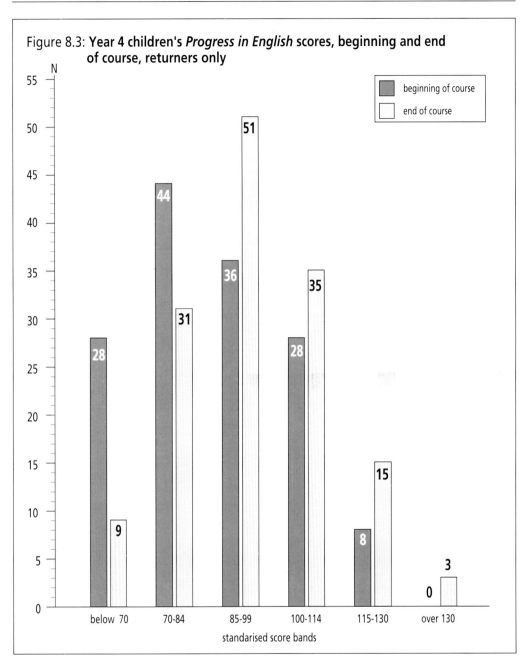

Figure 8.3: **Year 4 children's** *Progress in English* **scores, beginning and end of course, returners only**

For courses based in schools where the National Literacy Project was **not** operating, the gain on *Progress in English 9* can confidently be attributed to the Family Literacy courses, because it was statistically significantly greater than would be expected from normal schooling and development. Given this and the unlikelihood of its having a different cause, the gain in writing in these schools can also be attributed to the courses.

For courses based in schools where the National Literacy Project **was** operating, the gains cannot necessarily be attributed solely to the Family Literacy courses – here the

National Literacy Project was also contributing to children's development. Partitioning the gains is of course impossible, and would be invidious. It would be better to say that here the children received double benefit.

## 8.6  Conclusions on courses for families with a child in Year 4

- The Family Literacy approach was successfully adapted for families with a child in Year 4.

- The Year 4 parents were in general poorly qualified and not employed outside the home.

- The recruitment policy was largely successful, and depended mainly on personal contact. Good relations with host schools were also crucial.

- Attendance and retention rates (92 and 94 per cent respectively) were high for the children, and reasonably high for the parents (87 and 83 per cent respectively).

- The Year 4 parents significantly improved their literacy – their average final score was six per cent higher than the average starting score.

- Their tutors said the parents' confidence and ability to help their children had improved.

- Many of the parents planned to go on further courses, and some had gained employment.

- Some had become more involved with their children's schools.

- The children made substantial progress in writing and in literacy generally – the (strong) effect size of 0.58 represented about 14 months' gain in reading age in three months. The proportion who were struggling with literacy went down from 50 per cent to 28 per cent, while the proportion who were severely disadvantaged for learning went down from 19 per cent to 6 per cent.

- Boys and girls made approximately equal gains.

- **The gains for parents were close to those in the Demonstration Programmes, and the gains for children were directly comparable.**

## CHAPTER NINE

# Factors contributing to the success of programmes

Programme tutors were asked which factors they would identify as contributing to their Programme's success. As with the evaluation of the Demonstration Programmes, references were made to several factors which could be summarised as either **human factors** or material factors. Very similar issues emerged from the Linguistic Minorities and Year 4 models. Section 9.3 also summarises some challenges faced by the courses.

## 9.1  Human factors

Comments within this category focused on the following factors:

- *The calibre of the Programme staff*

- *The quality of the teaching offered*

- *What the parents themselves brought to the Programmes*

- *What the children brought*

- *The joint session.*

## 9.1.1 The calibre of the Programme staff

One issue raised was the close cooperation between Programme staff in terms of attitudes and approaches, and of their joint planning. Where this existed, both between the Programme tutors, and between tutors and any support assistants, tutors commented on the supportive nature of the partnerships, there was evidence of a *'team spirit'*. Equally important was the experience and efficiency of the Programme staff, teamed with their positive attitudes. Where staff were enthusiastic, and started out with the intention of making the Programme work, they were more likely to be successful. The quality of relationships was also highlighted, that between the tutors and the parents but equally that between the parents themselves. The informality and friendliness of Programme staff were crucial in making parents feel comfortable, '*... how you treat them, that's important.*'

Specifically raised by a Early Years tutor in one of the courses for linguistic minority families was the fact that she was a teacher in the school where the course was being run. This, she believed, saved time in the preparation stages (she could build up more of a relationship with the children and she was more aware of the school – how it functioned, its policies and syllabus), and allowed for a certain amount of follow-up that would not be possible with an outsider who would move on once the course drew to a close. The majority of the Programmes in this evaluation were, in fact, operating with children's tutors who were also teachers in the host schools.

## 9.1.2 The quality of the teaching offered

The nature of the Programme itself was identified as a factor contributing to its success. It was imaginative enough to be creatively adapted, so as to be able to offer individual attention and a whole range of different activities. One ABS tutor on a Year 4 course specifically referred to the word processing element of the adult teaching as being important. She believed that literacy by itself would not have the same '*pull*', especially the accreditation side of it.

Prior knowledge of Family Literacy through involvement in the Demonstration Programmes was highlighted by two tutors running Year 4 courses. This provided them with confidence in its outcomes, which in turn allowed them to '*sell it enthusiastically*' in schools.

Another factor, identified by an ABS tutor on a course for linguistic minority families, was feedback to parents on their children's progress. Without this, she felt, the parents would not continue attending. Sensitivity to parents' needs was acknowledged as an important factor and, within this, Programme staff running courses for linguistic minority families recognised the need to be sensitive to different cultures, in particular through the provision of course material which was pertinent and relevant to course members.

## 9.1.3 What the parents brought to the Programme

The commitment and support of the participating parents was recognised as an important feature in the success of the Programmes. Their subsequent growth in confidence then became a key component in that success. Finally, an ABS tutor on one of the courses for linguistic minority families recognised that, for many of the parents on the course, there was a social element involved. Actually getting out of the house was important to them, a factor which was influential in maintaining their attendance on the course.

## 9.1.4 What the children brought

Positive comments about the participating children were made by Programme staff operating both models. It was recognised that their eagerness and enthusiasm facilitated delivery of the course, and ensured few or no problems with behaviour. An ABS tutor on a course for linguistic minority families reflected on the children's enjoyment of, and very evident pride in, their parents' involvement in the course.

## 9.1.5 The joint session

The joint session was defined by several tutors as being a prime factor in the success of their Programme. For many parents, their motivation to attend was their desire to help their children and thus, for them, the joint session functioned as an embodiment of that desire. The parents themselves had been very positive about these sessions.

## 9.2 Material factors

Within this category, factors affecting the Programmes' success highlighted by the tutors included:

- Premises

- The support of the school and its senior management

- Effective recruitment/attendance and retention

- Time for planning and evaluation

- Accreditation

- Resources.

## 9.2.1 Premises

The provision of a room from which to operate the course was seen as a key component of its success. Several tutors acknowledged the siting of the course in school as a positive factor. It was seen as a familiar and non-threatening environment for parents. This issue was raised in particular by both tutors on one of the courses for linguistic minority families. Many of these parents, who were invariably women, would not have been able to attend had it been in any other location. School was seen as somewhere safe where male staff would not be perceived as a threat. Equally, no one in the family or the local community would gossip about them coming into school.

## 9.2.2 The support of the school and its senior management

Several tutors acknowledged the importance of the school's support and, in particular, that of its senior management. Again, this issue featured notably in the accounts of tutors running courses for linguistic minority families, where the courses' location in school was seen to be such an influential factor. Success was a more likely outcome in schools where staff understood the rationale underpinning the course and were positive towards it. A tutor on one of the Year 4 courses underlined this commitment where recruitment relied on the support of the school: *'. . . schools where they are able and prepared to put in a lot of effort with the parents, . . . are the ones where we have the most success.'*

### 9.2.3 Effective recruitment/attendance and retention

Recruitment was considered to be a factor in the success of Programmes where parents were made fully aware of exactly what the course entailed, and what they would be committing themselves to. In this way, attendance, and concomitantly retention, were more likely to be successful:

> *'I think the way that the project is sold to the parents is crucial, they have got to understand what they are committing themselves to at the beginning. . . , and not have any preconceptions which don't fit the model, I think if it's made clear that this is what the objective is, this is what we intend doing and that they know that that's what the model is, that's really important, so that part of the way through they are not going to say "Well this isn't what I thought it was going to be" and sort of disappear, I think that's really important.'* (Year 4 course ABS tutor)

### 9.2.4 Time for planning and evaluation

Time for planning and evaluation was perceived by tutors to be a factor which had an important bearing on the success of a Programme.

### 9.2.5 Accreditation

An ABS tutor on one of the Year 4 courses believed that the accreditation was a factor in the Programmes' success. The fact that there was no pressure on the parents meant that most of them did actually complete what was necessary in order to achieve the accreditation. At the same time, it was all so closely linked to their children's education and this, combined with the informal approach of the tutors, kept them interested and motivated. Interestingly, accreditation was also raised by tutors again in terms of challenges affecting the implementation of the Programmes – see the next section.

### 9.2.6 Resources

Money for materials and resources was highlighted by tutors as being influential in the effectiveness of the Programmes.

## 9.3  Possible barriers or challenges to the success of the Programmes

Tutors on each of the courses were asked to indicate what they perceived to be the major challenges affecting the implementation of the Programme. Once again, the factors highlighted were similar across the two models.

Challenges highlighted by the tutors related to the following:

- Relationships

- The teaching

- Assessment and accreditation

- Time

- Commitment of the schools.

### 9.3.1 Relationships

Relationships were raised as an issue which could cause problems. That between the tutors and the parents was important: parents had to recognise the advantages of learning about, and taking on board, a system that was probably very different from their own experience. For some, actually settling down to work was problematic when they had not done anything like that for several years. The ABS tutor on a course for linguistic minority families emphasised the need to help the group gel in the early stages of the course. She believed it was worth devoting some time to this issue to avoid losing any parents who felt uncomfortable.

### 9.3.2 The teaching

Several comments relating to the actual teaching being a challenge were made by tutors. The organisation of the teaching programme was difficult at first, particularly for those tutors with no prior knowledge of such courses. For some it had been very much a case of working from one week to the next, rather than to an established framework. Working with parents at different levels was challenging; there could be several parents working on different things, all wanting the tutor's attention. Ensuring access to appropriate materials could then also be a problem. At the same time, being creative and ensuring that the course kept participants motivated was recognised as an important, albeit challenging, factor. For the children, especially the very young ones, it was sometimes difficult to keep the momentum going as they became quite tired.

Finally, in this section, tutors reflected on the difficulty of achieving a balance in the teaching. An ABS tutor on a course for linguistic minority families recognised that their course was probably weighted more towards activities relating to the child, whereas other courses might spend more time working directly on the parents' literacy.

### 9.3.3 Assessment and accreditation

Several ABS tutors felt that it was very difficult, in the time allowed, to create opportunities for assessment towards accreditation for the parents. The attempt to do this resulted in constant pressure to complete work. The idea of working towards accreditation was something that often had to be introduced very carefully because it was such a daunting prospect for many parents. One ABS tutor on a Year 4 course went so far as to describe it as being '... *almost a barrier to learning'*. Parents often reacted quite negatively to being assessed; many had not been involved with education since leaving school themselves, and school may well have been a negative experience for some.

The assessment of the children was felt by many of their tutors to be inappropriate. The children on the courses were those who were not achieving for whatever reason, and thus the focus was necessarily on building up their skills and confidence. Several of the tutors believed that the initial assessment was just too difficult for them, and therefore would have an adverse effect. An ABS tutor on one of the Year 4 courses, who referred to assessment for both adults and children as *'a major stumbling block'*, suggested as an improvement a different model of assessment for the children, based on tasks at which they could achieve. She surmised that this would still provide an indication of skill levels, but the children would actually be achieving.

### 9.3.4 Time

Time constraints were nominated as a barrier to success. It was a constant challenge to complete the work required at the standard at which the tutors would like to see it done. There was often a need to prioritise to ensure that, whilst trying to include what people had indicated a preference for, it was also important. Children's tutors on both a Year 4 course and one for linguistic minority families referred to the ongoing juggling of course and host school teaching commitments.

### 9.3.5 Commitment of the schools

A lack of commitment of the schools involved was sometimes seen as a barrier to success. It was vital that all concerned were committed to the Programme, and the support of the headteacher was paramount. Even so, lack of communication within a school was sometimes a problem.

An ABS tutor on a Year 4 course was concerned to see the initiative become embedded in schools so that it could really become successful and go some way towards raising standards, in the classroom as well as in families. This view was endorsed in the additional comments made by an ABS tutor on one of the courses for linguistic minority families, who advocated an ongoing programme of such courses in schools where there was a need. In this way, she believed, the initiative would become embedded and parents would naturally come to perceive it as the norm.

## 9.4 Conclusion

Overall, the comments from course tutors were positive, in spite of the challenges mentioned in the previous section. They had enjoyed running the courses and had much to reflect on now in hindsight which they could build on in order to set up future courses. Most felt they had built up resources and experience and had done something for the confidence and learning of course participants. One ABS tutor encapsulated this positive attitude by enthusing *'I am definitely an advocate.'*

## CHAPTER TEN

# Evidence from the observation of teaching sessions

Note on orthographic convention: Quotations from interviews with course staff are presented in *italics*; quotations from the observers' notes in Roman.

Observations of teaching sessions were conducted during the four terms from Spring 1997 to Spring 1998. Observations were conducted at 11 linguistic minority or Year 4 centres, and 32 sessions were observed. Teachers' comments on the observed sessions were gathered, together with relevant documentation. Most of the teachers thought the sessions that had been observed were typical sessions. On only a very few occasions did teachers report any variations attributable to the presence of an observer.

## 10.1 Planning

The observers noted that every one of the courses had been quite carefully planned, but each was planned quite differently. The informing principles that staff brought to their course planning differed widely: some chose to devise a structure embracing all three types of session, others worked from a less complex linear progression for each type, whilst yet others relied on progression through a task over a period of time as their informing principle. Within these differing structures, there were differently formulated links between the three types of session, but in most of the plans, a dominant principle was that the parental sessions should provide preparation for the joint sessions with the children. The children's sessions were not always planned to link with the other two, sometimes retaining a quite distinct autonomy of remediation and support.

The following is an example of quite complex course planning (on a programme for linguistic minority families). Three themes – the child's world, the outside world, and creative work – equally divided a nine-week course. Each theme had a limited but appropriate list of topics associated with it, and some distinct activities – handwriting, drawing, speaking rhymes and storybook reading – were planned to be part of all three themes. Work for each week was set out on an A4 grid designed to express the relationship between the three different types of session within each week. The continuity and progression through the nine-week course could thus be gained either for a type of session or for all three sessions by turning the nine A4 pages.

LEAs bidding for the scheme provide a programme structure for participating centres. Some LEAs extended this approach by mounting induction sessions for the adult and children's tutors who were selected to run the courses. These sessions were described by one LEA adviser as 'invaluable'. During the sessions, tutors from different centres were able to get together to plan their courses.

## 10.2 Clarity of objectives

The observation reports indicated that in nearly all cases the teachers made clear what were to be the objectives of the session, either at the beginning or at appropriate points as the session progressed. In the few sessions where this was not observed it was because the structure of the programme or some form of routine familiarity had made evident to the pupils what was expected of them. Generally, teachers were likely to explain in advance the ultimate goals for a session in those sessions where adults were present. Children, especially younger children, were presented with more local goals.

There were a few other occasions where clear initial explanation was not evident, however. In one, it had been deliberately concealed. In this series of two sessions, a teacher had been working from practising cursive squiggles with the children through pictures and writing in the joint session about what 'My Mummy Likes' (with all the cursive practice involved in writing 'Mummy') towards the teacher quickly and expertly producing a class book which became the reading focus at the end of the session. Concealing her intention initially enabled the teacher to achieve an effective and quite dramatic conclusion to the joint session.

The means teachers used to achieve this clarity were largely similar across centres. Their explanation was simple and straightforward. Where they could rely upon the familiarity of an established routine, or upon a continuing activity, they did. If not, they made use of key words on flipcharts or wallboards to reinforce their explanations. In instances where the objective was the production of an artefact, teachers often strategically introduced at some time during the session a previously-constructed model as an example. These straightforward approaches to explanation and introduction normally led to orderly sessions. Probably significantly, on one of the few occasions where any kind of disorder was reported and where discipline was difficult, the opening did not appear to rely on any of these means.

## 10.3 Use of resources

A range of resources were available. The observations seemed to show that the majority of teachers relied on the traditional resources of pen (now felt tip), paper, and wall board (now sometimes a flipchart). It should be said, however, that word processors were available to, and used at, all of the centres, even though not many were in use during the observed visits. Their ultimate use at the centres seemed to be the production of materials that resulted from the course, in at least one case to produce publicity materials for the next course.

The range and style of course-produced resources are much more noteworthy than a simple count of materials used in a session. There was a wide variety of sometimes ingeniously apposite worksheets that had been devised for the courses and, on many courses, the production of scrapbooks and other artefacts led to extremely apposite aids to learning which the parents could use. At one centre the observers saw how, with a fold and a snip, sheets of A4 paper could be transformed into a durable little booklet. Other craft activities included the following:

In a joint session with nursery children and their parents present, the children's copying of writing strokes on A4 paper rapidly became a carded, laminated, wipe-clean sampler that each family could take home to use to assist the child's mastery of cursive script.

Arguably the most ambitiously crafted artefact was in preparation at a centre where the headteacher's husband was a DT specialist who had previously come in to do a workshop with the parents looking at pop-up mechanisms. In the observed session the group members were about to make a book of the story of the *Three Little Pigs*. Each page would have the children's text on one side and a pop-up mechanism on the other. The parents were to use the word processor to set out their child's part of the story and then create an illustrative pop-up mechanism on the other side of the page.

## 10.4 Management of learning

There seemed to be few problems of classroom management in the observed sessions. There was only one session, a children-only session with year 4 children, where issues of control overtook the planned session.

One teacher commented on general issues of the management of learning in young children, namely seeking to maximise and maintain the learner's interest and to minimise any stress:

> '*I thought it went quite well, we did all the things we planned to do. As I said before, although we've got different activities, by the time you get to the end of the session, the children are losing interest and concentration and getting very tired. So the activities we did after the break were less successful than the ones we did before the break in some ways, because they'd made the jigsaw and then they were losing interest. The tape I think actually revived their interest a little bit, then we needed to move on so we did the games.*'

The observers did not report any sessions where individual students did not learn anything, but the teachers were asked related questions, one of which was about students who found the work difficult. Because they had a greater knowledge than the observers about their students, they could identify students with difficulty more readily and more precisely than the observers.

## 10.5 Differentiation

The ability range in some groups of parents was very broad, and this sometimes posed challenges. For example one ABS tutor commented:

> '*Yes, two of the less able, one woman doesn't write in Urdu and she doesn't write in English, she never went to school. I thought she was going to drop out because everybody else is so able.*'

This teacher had decided to adopt a cautious strategy towards the assessment of her student:

> '*I'm very aware that she is embarrassed, it took me ages to test her because I fed it in very gently. I know for her to sit down and write something for me is nearly impossible. I think she's in with the group now so I'm not so worried but for the first two or three weeks until the group gels, you can lose people.*'

The adult groups in Linguistic Minority courses were more likely to demonstrate a wider range of ability, since some parents (as in the example above) who enrolled had not, as children in their native land, attended school and might, as a consequence, be illiterate in their first language as well as having little command of English. But the issue of diverse ability was present on nearly all Family Literacy programmes, and had attendant management implications:

> *'I think when there is such a big range and you have got people who struggle like that ... I think for the occasional parents who are really dyslexic ... I suppose it is very difficult to cater for (them) at all because their needs are so specific. It's not even just that they are slow to pick it all up, it's that their needs are quite specific. A lot of it (the course programme) they obviously can take part in, but it's always been very hard (to plan and manage) and I don't know if I have improved on it at all really or managed to find a way round differentiating the activities more successfully, so that people pick what they would be comfortable with.'*

In children's sessions the usual support that teachers provided, as noted by the observers, was differentially to help those with most apparent need, making sure each understood what was required, tailoring any requirement, if it proved necessary, to the child's abilities, and offering constant encouragement. Reported comments are of the kind:

> (The teacher) gave plenty of help and support to the children during the session. She gauged her questions on the story very much to the ability of the children. Equally, when (the children were) looking for their names (concealed) around the classroom, she made sure that those who needed more help were given it. She moved around all the time in the craft activity giving help where needed but equally, was firm when she had to be, for example in encouraging two of the boys who kept saying they could not do it.

Support in the parents-only sessions similarly aimed to differentiate where necessary and to ensure constant encouragement. But the goal of the encouragement seemed different: with the children the usual aim was to give the children the social and conceptual skills to make progress in their school work. With the adults, teachers sought activities to give their parent/students confidence in what they could already achieve, and to show them how all could capitalise on those achievements to help their children.

The other marked difference between the parents-only and children-only sessions was that the former were frequently described as 'relaxed'; the teachers usually seemed to adopt a brisker approach to learning with the children.

These two differences combined to create a 'can do' feeling in a relaxed environment, and indicate that the planning of the approach and the atmosphere of the parents-only sessions were generally appropriate for the parents following them.

# 10.6 The joint sessions

Most courses were planned so that the parents-only and children-only sessions were planned to provide and support joint-session activity. The parents were using their developing skills to assist their children's immediate understanding, and seemed likely to be able to assist their children's learning in the future.

General indicators of the effectiveness of the joint sessions were:

- the enjoyment of parents and children in what was, for some, newly found modes and means of communication

- the growing appreciation, especially marked in the Linguistic Minority courses, by the children of what their parents could offer to their school learning

- the obvious joint sense of achievement of a task completed

- the shared enjoyment of a co-operative performance activity.

There was plenty of evidence of effective interaction between parents and children in the joint sessions. The eight comments on joint session activity which follow are representative. They have been taken from the observation schedules, and seem to indicate that, for this sort of work, the most obviously effective interaction occurs in sessions where the teacher starts by modelling the activity for parents, and then hands over to them. The more practical the focus of the work, the easier it apparently becomes for the teacher to do so:

> The different activities in the session were introduced by the tutors but then, the nature of them, being very practical and craft based, meant that the tutors acted as facilitators. There was plenty of interaction between children and the adult with whom they were working, but not so much between other children and adults.

> The interaction was excellent throughout. The tutor initiated the activities, but the parents were able to mediate each with their children. This led to a great deal of parent/child interaction.

> The changeover from written activity to practical activity was initiated by the children's teacher. After that, parents very much took the initiative in the mobile making, only referring to the tutors if they had a particular problem.

> (The tutor) began leading the session but then split everyone up into small groups. When they came back into the large group she acted as facilitator so that the groups could feed back what they had done.

After the paired reading, (the tutor) led the session to begin with then everyone began to work in pairs or small groups on their worksheets. (The tutor) encouraged the children to contribute as much as possible to any discussion work that took place.

The session was tutor-led to begin with but then activities were introduced, interspersed with more input from the librarians. Everybody was encouraged to contribute to the session. (This was an observation of a library visit.)

Although the main bulk of the session was the reading of the play, everyone could contribute if they wished. The children's teacher did ask questions about the story as they went along which sometimes triggered off discussion. Both children were quite at ease with the tutors and with both parents.

Because the bulk of the joint session involved a listening activity, there was not much opportunity for students to contribute. It became clear though that people were used to making contributions once the activity was finished.

## 10.7 Participation during separate sessions

In the parents-only and children-only sessions the participation took a different form. In almost all of the sessions observed, it is clear that the teachers still encouraged participation, through either communication with them, or amongst the students themselves. But it is equally clear that the teachers were more conscious than in the joint sessions that instruction/transmission was their primary function. As a result, most of these sessions took on a more formal atmosphere. But they did not become excessively formal because of the level of secondary, parent/parent and (to a lesser extent) child/child, communication that was encouraged.

## 10.8 Record-keeping

Approaches to record-keeping, and generally keeping track of what course members were achieving, were markedly different both within and across courses.

There were, however, tendencies shared by most courses. A frequently-used means of keeping track of work was in the form of a personal file, and:

- work from the children-only sessions was normally kept in a file, either at the base or in the child's own classroom

- work from the parents-only sessions was also kept in a file, but the parents more frequently retained possession of the file so as to enable them to do work at home

- work from the joint sessions was most usually practical and was either taken home to be used, or displayed in the base.

Another useful, productive, and quite commonly used method of keeping track for the adults sessions was to review at the end of each session what had been attempted and achieved during the session and for each student to make a personal record of that achievement.

For all courses the record of the children's work needed to be diagnostic as well as documentary. The teachers approached this responsibility in various ways, ranging from very informal jottings in a notebook – this with a small group of children who were working with the teacher who was their normal nursery teacher – to routine weekly summaries of progress carefully documenting evidence of progression.

In some courses, especially those where the parents were working towards a form of qualification, e.g. Wordpower, records of their work and of evidence of new skills they had demonstrated were kept quite formally.

There was also considerable variation in the way that the children's work and progress was reported to and discussed with the children's class teachers. But most usually, at least during the progress of the course, this did not seem to be formalised in any way. At most centres, teachers normally seemed to rely on joint, informal, conversation as the way to share comments with the other. Only during one visit was there reference to work completed on the course being passed to the class teacher so that it might be recorded in the child's achievement folder.

An example of one of the least formal approaches to keeping track of the children's progress was:

*'It's just generally by keeping an eye on them every week, checking that they have filled in their book review and they have done a little bit more work on their scrap book. The diary we did last week I will collect that in because invariably it goes missing.'*

More systematic processes of keeping track can be seen in the following observations:

> The children had pupil files into which their work went. Pupil observations were done weekly and end of course summary notes went in with their half term reports. (Teacher's name) did half-termly and termly reports. She also prepared reports for the class teacher and met with her each week to discuss what she could usefully focus on.

> At the beginning of the course the parents were asked to write what they expected to get from the course. She (the teacher) then assessed them to see what stage each was at. She did individual learning programmes for them with short-term goals and which skills they needed to work on. She kept progress sheets which were filled in after each session showing three sections for the date, the work done and comments. A record sheet of the short joint sessions and of the parents-only sessions was done weekly, noting how they had gone and recording any comments. The overall assessment done was the Basic Skills Agency's *Assessing Progress in Basic Skills* and she kept records of all this.

## 10.9 Conclusions from observations of teaching sessions

The courses for linguistic minority families and those with a child in Year 4 showed evidence of a range of factors which contributed to their effectiveness:

- Careful and integrated joint planning

- Clear explanation of objectives to participants

- Effective use of resources

- Good management and differentiation of learning

- Excellent learning and participation in joint sessions

- Careful record-keeping.

In our view, all of these factors contributed powerfully to the success of these two models.

## CHAPTER ELEVEN

# Conclusions and recommendations

_____

## 11.1 The three Alternative Models overall

- The attempt to adapt the original Family Literacy model for families with a child in Year 7 was largely unsuccessful.

- But the original model was successfully adapted both for linguistic minority families with a child aged 3 to 6, and for families with a child in Year 4.

## 11.2 The linguistic minorities model

- The main linguistic minority recruited was speakers of Urdu and Punjabi.

- The recruitment policy was largely successful, and depended mainly on personal contact.

- Attendance and retention rates were high for the children, and reasonably high for the parents.

- The parents significantly improved their literacy in English.

- The parents gained confidence both generally and in their command of spoken and written English.

- The parents' ability to help their children had improved.

- Many of the parents planned to go on further courses.

- Many had become more involved with their children's schools.

- The children made substantial progress in writing and in early literacy generally – effect size = 0.72.

- Both their Early Years tutors and their school teachers said the children's fluency in spoken English had improved.

## 11.3 The Year 4 model

- The recruitment policy was largely successful, and depended mainly on personal contact. Good relations with host schools were also crucial.

- Attendance and retention rates were reasonably high for both parents and children.

- The parents significantly improved their literacy.

- The parents gained in confidence and in ability to help their children.

- Many of the parents planned to go on further courses, and some had gained employment.

- Some had become more involved with their children's schools.

- The children made substantial progress in writing and in literacy generally – effect size = 0.58.

## 11.4 Material factors in the two models' success

The material factors which were cited by the tutors as contributing to the Programmes' success included premises, the support of the host school and its senior management and staff, effective recruitment/attendance and retention, time for planning and evaluation, accreditation, and resources.

## 11.5 Human factors in the two models' success

- The calibre of the Programme staff – in particular, their close cooperation and joint planning.

- The quality of the teaching offered – it was imaginative and attractive.

- What the parents themselves brought to the Programmes – especially commitment and support.

- What the children brought – eagerness and enthusiasm.

- The joint session – which, as in the Demonstration Programmes, was the motor of the courses' success because of the opportunities it provided for parents and children to work together in a productive and (for some) unfamiliar manner.

## 11.6 Possible barriers to success

Challenges highlighted by the course tutors related to the following:

- Relationships, especially 'inducting' the parents.

- The teaching – keeping on top of the changing demands of the work.

- Assessment and accreditation, which was sometimes felt as inappropriate and too demanding for both parents and children.

- Time constraints.

- Commitment of the schools – which need to take it on board to ensure that the success is spread.

## 11.7 Conclusions from observations of teaching sessions

The courses for linguistic minority families and those with a child in Year 4 showed evidence of a range of factors which contributed to their effectiveness:

- Careful and integrated joint planning

- Clear explanation of objectives to participants

- Effective use of resources

- Good management and differentiation of learning

- Excellent learning and participation in joint sessions

- Careful record-keeping.

## 11.8 Lessons and recommendations

- Attempts to improve the basic skills of low attainers in secondary schools should take a quite different approach – such as that already adopted by the Basic Skills Agency in its Innovative Development Projects.

- The success of the linguistic minorities model shows that the original model can be successfully implemented with different linguistic/ethnic groups. This preventive approach is not only successful but welcomed.

- The success of the Year 4 model shows that the original model can be successfully implemented at that point in the primary age range; but these courses need even more careful ground-laying and planning than those for the younger age range, because of the greater complexity and pressure of the timetable in Year 4, and the existence of other initiatives at that point (especially the National Literacy Strategy).

- The Early Years and Year 4 models should therefore continue to be widely disseminated.

- Providers need further convincing of the need for assessment, and to be provided with efficient means for doing so.

- Good personal relations are key to much of the work: in successful recruitment, in cooperation between course staff, and in collaborating with host schools.

- The key factor in staffing is the calibre of staff.

- The key factor in teaching is the joint sessions, to which good planning and teaching in the separate sessions build up.

- All these factors contribue to the educational coherence of the approach.

- These essential features of the original model therefore need to be retained, and dilutions of that model should be resisted.

# References

Basic Skills Agency (1997). *Assessing Progress in Basic Skills: Literacy*. London: Basic Skills Agency.

Brooks, G., Flanagan, N., Henkhuzens, Z. and Hutchison, D. (1998). *What Works for Slow Readers? The Effectiveness of Early Intervention Schemes*. Slough: NFER.

Brooks, G., Gorman, T.P., Harman, J., Hutchison, D., Kinder, K., Moor, H. and Wilkin, A. (1997). *Family Literacy Lasts: The NFER Follow-up Study of the Basic Skills Agency's Demonstration Programmes*. London: Basic Skills Agency.

Brooks, G., Gorman, T.P., Harman, J., Hutchison, D. and Wilkin, A. (1996). *Family Literacy Works: The NFER Evaluation of the Basic Skills Agency's Family Literacy Demonstration Programmes*. London: Basic Skills Agency.

Brooks, G. and Keys, W. (1998). 'Headteacher's views on English in the Primary School.' *NFER Annual Survey of Trends in Education, Digest no.6*. Slough: NFER.

Gorman, T.P. (1996). Assessing Young Children's Writing: Supplementary Notes and Scripts. (mimeographed) Slough: NFER.

Gorman, T.P. and Brooks, G. (1996). *Assessing Young Children's Writing: A Step by Step Guide*. London: Basic Skills Agency.

Kispal, A., Hagues, N. and Ruddock, G. (1994). *Progress in English 8-13. Tests and Teacher's Guides*. Windsor: NFER-Nelson.

Sainsbury, M. (1998). *Literacy Hours: a Survey of the National Picture in the Spring Term of 1998*. Slough: NFER.

Vincent, D., Crumpler, M. and de la Mare, M. (1996). *Reading Progress Tests. Manual for Stage One of the Reading Progress Tests*. London: Hodder and Stoughton. (Includes *Literacy Baseline*)

# Full Description of how the Evaluation was Carried Out

## A.1 Forms of information

The forms of information gathered by NFER in this study were as shown in Table A.1.

Table A.1: **Forms of information gathered**

| Quantitative data | | Qualitative data |
|---|---|---|
| on parents: | background information<br>literacy attainment | interviews with Adult Basic Skills (ABS) tutors and with teachers (Early Years, Year 4 or Year 7, according to Model) observations of teaching sessions |
| on children: | background information<br>reading attainment<br>writing attainment | |

## A.2 Frequency of quantitative data collection

Background information on parents and children was gathered once, near the beginning of the course, on the four 'cohorts' beginning courses in the Spring, Summer and Autumn terms of 1997 and the Spring term of 1998. All the other forms of quantitative data were gathered both near the beginning and just before the end of the course for each of the four cohorts of participants. Thus across the four cohorts there were eight occasions on which quantitative data were gathered. All quantitative data were gathered on NFER's behalf by course staff.

## A.3 Quantitative data-collection instruments

### A.3.1 Background information

Background information on parents was collected through an Adult Profile form covering sex, date of birth, ethnic group, occupational status, first and any other languages, highest qualification, and whether the parent had received basic skills tuition before. A similar Child Profile form covered sex, date of birth, ethnic group and languages. Information on family structures was not collected.

## A.3.2 Parents' literacy

In the Demonstration Programmes, parents had been asked to provide separate evidence on their reading and writing attainment, in the form of their responses to (respectively) a cloze test and a three-part writing task. The cloze test was used for reading partly for reasons of practicality, and partly because the Programme Coordinators thought it would be accessible to the parents. However, there are widespread doubts about cloze tests, because they have very little resemblance to real-life reading tasks. Also, after the Demonstration Programmes evaluation, the Agency published an instrument, *Assessing Progress in Basic Skills: Literacy* (Basic Skills Agency, 1997) which had much greater content validity than cloze tests and covered both reading and writing. This instrument was therefore chosen to provide estimates of the parents' literacy attainments. It was administered by the ABS tutors, who then sent the results to NFER.

No general assessment was carried out of the parents' attainment or progress in spoken English, partly because such assessment is time-consuming if it is to be valid, and partly because no standard measures of adults' oral skills exist. Staff on the linguistic minority programmes did point out at the beginning of the evaluation that not assessing the oral skills of people for whom English is an additional language could underestimate their progress. Staff on those courses were therefore encouraged to carry out such assessments locally, and to report progress in spoken English to the Basic Skills Agency and NFER alongside progress in literacy. The diversity of local instruments used for this purpose meant, however, that no generalisation of results could be achieved for spoken English, and such results are not reported.

## A.3.3 Children's literacy

Information on children's reading and writing attainment was gathered for NFER by their Family Literacy teachers.

### *Reading*

In the Demonstration Programmes evaluation, for assessing 'reading', a group of Early Years teachers were trained to administer the *Reading Recognition* subtest of the *Peabody Individual Achievement Tests* (PIAT). When that evaluation began, this was the only reading test standardised on British children as young as five. It could have been re-used in this study, and with all three age groups, since its norms extend to age 12 (and well beyond). However, it is individually administered and therefore time-consuming. For this study, therefore, it was decided to use standardised (norm-referenced) group tests, and to use a different, age-appropriate, one for each age group.

71

For linguistic minority children the test chosen was the *Literacy Baseline* within the *Reading Progress Tests* (Vincent, Crumpler and de la Mare, 1996). This test covers a suitable range of emerging and early literacy skills, can be administered to small groups of children, and is standardised for the age range 5:00-6:04. At the discretion of their teachers, children who were thought to be too young to be assessed on the *Literacy Baseline* were not given this test. Within the group of children who were given the test, standardised scores were calculated for all those whose ages were within the range of the norms both at the beginning and the end of the course (therefore effectively those who were aged between 5:00 and 6:01 at the beginning), and the average standardised score for that subsample is given in this report. Raw scores were available for all the children who were given the test, and the average raw score is reported for that whole group (which includes those for whom standardised scores were available).

For children in Years 4 and 7 the tests chosen were respectively *Progress in English 9* and *Progress in English 12* (Kispal, Hagues and Ruddock, 1994). These are also standardised group tests, and each covers not only reading but also other aspects of literacy, such as spelling. In particular, each level incorporates suggestions for writing tasks (though scores on these are not counted into the calculation of the standardised scores). Standardised scores were available for all the Year 4 and Year 7 children who took the relevant test.

### Writing

In the Demonstration Programmes evaluation, for 'writing', the Early Years teachers asked the children to produce a few lines or a sentence if they could, or if not their own name and some other letters, or if not that then letter-like forms or scribbles, or if not that then a copy of a few words, or if not that then a drawing. The objective was to elicit at each stage the most advanced form of emergent or early writing which the child could produce *independently.*

This approach was retained and strengthened for the linguistic minority children in this evaluation. The Early Years teachers in these courses were given the same instructions as in the original evaluation; those instructions were by then incorporated in the book (Gorman and Brooks, 1996) which arose from the original evaluation. The Early Years teachers were also sent further guidance notes (Gorman, 1996) expanding the analysis in Gorman and Brooks (1996).

This approach was not suitable for assessing the writing of children in Years 4 and 7. Instead, their Family Literacy teachers were asked to set their pupils one of the writing tasks in the appropriate level of *Progress in English*, and then to impression-mark their pupils' scripts on a rising 7-point scale (1 = low, 4 = midpoint, 7 = high). The teachers were sent guidance on this, and this guidance in turn referred to the notes in the *Progress in English Teacher's Guides.*

For all three ages of children involved, the assessments of writing reported here are (inescapably) based on raw scores.

## A.4 Quantitative data collected

The numbers of LEAs, courses, parents and children providing quantitative date were as shown in Table A.2.

Table A.2: **Numbers of LEAs, courses, parents and children providing quantitative data, by Model and overall**

|  | Model | | | Total |
|---|---|---|---|---|
|  | Linguistic minorities | Year 4 | Year 7 |  |
| LEAs | 7 | 7 | 6 | 18* |
| Courses | 22 | 17 | 8 | 47 |
| Parents | | | | |
| - profiles | 166 | 142 | 41 | 349 |
| - tested at beginning & end | 163 | 115 | 9 | 287 |
| Children | | | | |
| - profiles | 160 | 126 | 30 | 316 |
| - tested at beginning & end | 170 | 147 | 27 | 344 |

*Because two LEAs provided data on two Models, the total number of LEAs providing data was not 20 but 18.

The figure for linguistic minority children tested is the number who were given the writing task, and the numbers who were tested on the *Literacy Baseline* were smaller, because some of the youngest children in the study were not given this test.

Table A.2 shows that the amount of data collected on linguistic minority and Year 4 courses was adequate. However, the amount collected on Year 7 courses was very small – this is discussed in section A.6 below.

## A.5 Qualitative data

Qualitative data were gathered in each of the four terms. The interviews with tutors and teachers were conducted by four NFER researchers, and were based on a semi-structured schedule. This covered recruitment, teaching (both approach and content), the staff's own opinions of the effectiveness of various aspects of the Programmes, relationships with 'host' schools (including any feedback on children who had been in a Programme), the Agency's model of family literacy, and benefits to parents and children. For staff on linguistic minority courses only, the schedule included several specific questions on bilingual issues.

Observations of teaching sessions were also carried out by the NFER researchers using a schedule which covered:

- detailed observation of each session

- evaluative comment on each session observed

- discussion with the teachers responsible for the courses

- the collection of relevant documentation.

In all, 15 fieldwork visits were made, six to linguistic minority LEAs, five to Year 4 LEAs, and four to Year 7 LEAs. On each visit, the ABS tutor and the children's teacher (Early Years, Year 4 or Year 7, as appropriate) was interviewed. Also, three teaching sessions were observed: one parents-only, one children-only, and one joint.

## A.6 Comment on the evaluation of Year 7 courses

As pointed out earlier in this Appendix, the amount of quantitative data gathered on Year 7 courses was very small. This was mainly because rather few such courses were actually run, which in turn appears to have been due to the difficulty of recruiting parents onto Year 7 courses. Staff on such courses who were interviewed emphasised how difficult recruitment had been – and these were people who had actually managed to get courses started. It is known that many other attempts to establish Year 7 courses were not successful.

The difficulty of recruiting parents of Year 7 children was compounded by the even greater difficulty of retaining them. Three of the LEAs which did run Year 7 courses provided, between them, course reports on four such courses; the average attendance of parents on these courses was 49 per cent. On fieldwork visits too, parents were often noticeable by their absence. In one supposedly 'joint' session on a Year 7 course observed by the Project Director, seven children and eight adults were present – but only two of the adults were parents of those children. The rest were course staff and local literacy volunteers. This was therefore not in any justifiable sense a *family* literacy event, but a literacy support class for children with problems.

On the quantitative side of the evaluation, the outcome of the small numbers on Year 7 courses was that

- for the parents, the statistical significance of the test results could not be calculated;

- for the children, the difference between their average scores for the beginning and the end of the course was non-significant.

There is therefore no quantitative evidence that the Year 7 model was effective.

We therefore conclude that **the attempt to adapt the original Family Literacy model for families with a child in Year 7 was largely unsuccessful.**